50 LESSONS FOR WOMEN LAWYERS FROM WOMEN LAWYERS

OTHER BOOKS BY NORA RIVA BERGMAN

50 Lessons for Lawyers: Earn more. Stress less. Be awesome.
Available at amazon.com, Barnes & Noble, and as a Kindle book.

COMING SOON

50 Lessons for Mindful Lawyers
50 Lessons for Happy Lawyers

50 LESSONS FOR WOMEN LAWYERS FROM WOMEN LAWYERS

Career and Life Lessons From 50 Successful Women Lawyers

NORA RIVA BERGMAN

ISBN-13: 978-0-9972637-1-8
ISBN-13: 978-0-9972637-2-5
Library of Congress Control Number 2019902671
Berroco Canyon Publishing, Tarpon Springs, Florida

TABLE OF CONTENTS

ACKNOWLEDGEMENTS

"Thank you" is the best prayer that anyone could say. I say that one a lot.
Thank you expresses extreme gratitude, humility, understanding.

— ALICE WALKER

This book simply would not have been possible without our contributors. I owe a huge "Thank you" to each and every woman who has shared her story in this book. I know that the willingness of our contributors to share the good, the bad, the wonderful, the painful, and the empowering lessons of their lives will inspire other women lawyers to reflect on their own lives—and perhaps give them the courage to make a change for the better.

I'd like to especially thank Michelle Suskauer and Julee Milham. Michelle was one of the first people I reached out to when I got the idea for this book. Her enthusiastic support motivated me to take those first few steps. There is a saying that "the journey of a thousand miles begins with a single step." Thank you, Michelle, for inspiring me to take that first step. Julee has been a friend and trusted advisor since shortly after I graduated from law school. She was instrumental in helping me put the legal pieces of this puzzle together. I would never have been able to continue the journey without Julee's support and wise counsel.

I'd also like to thank my creative director, Brian Frolo. Brian's creative talent is visible everywhere. He designed the *50 Lessons for Lawyers* logo and the cover of this book. Brian is the brains behind my website, www.reallifeprac-tice.com and created www.50LessonsForWomenLawyers.com. Thank you, Brian, for all you do for me. Thank you to our editor, David Wasserstrom, who worked diligently to edit the lessons in this book with a focus on letting each woman speak in her own voice. His comments and insights throughout the editing process were invaluable.

Finally, I'd like to thank the team that supports me in all the work I do. Cindy Moore has been my assistant since 2008. Without her, I would not have been able to serve my clients and bring this book to fruition. Thank you, Cindy. Melody Jones is my marketing assistant and manages much of my social media. Thank you, Melody, for helping me stay on top of everything social. And thank you to my team at JKS Publications, Angelle Barbazon and Sara Wigel, for their advice and direction throughout the creation of this book.

● ● ● ●

INTRODUCTION

Reading is the key that opens doors to many good things in life.
Reading shaped my dreams, and more reading helped me make
my dreams come true.

− RUTH BADER GINSBURG

I hope that this book helps you to open doors to many good things in life, to shape (or reshape) your dreams, and to help you make those dreams come true. Our dreams and goals always start as just a thought—just an idea. This book is a tangible example of a dream coming true—an idea coming to life.

I had the idea for a book that would become a handbook for women lawyers at every stage of their careers. And I knew that, as women lawyers, there is so much we can learn from one another. My vision is that the Lessons in this book shared by the incredible women who have lived them will be a starting point for conversations that will help other women lawyers realize their dreams, regardless of where they are in their lives or careers. So, while the idea for this book was mine, the ideas in it are not. The 50 Lessons are the ideas and stories from a diverse group of women. The contributors include women practicing in large firms and sole practitioners; women in private and public practice; current and former national, state, and local bar association presidents; judges; law school professors; entrepreneurs; and other published authors.

We are at an inflection point in the legal profession. We are at a place where women can have a tremendously positive influence on the practice and business of law. Sharing our stories of successes and challenges – and providing not only advice, but affirmation that so much of what we feel and have experienced has been felt and experienced by others – can be truly transformational.

The practice of law is grounded in transformation. Law transforms culture and society, and lawyers transform people's lives each day. Whether that transformation comes in the challenge of closing a business deal for a client or helping someone navigate the challenges in the breakup of a family or the death of a loved one, it is transformation, nonetheless. When women bring their whole selves to these challenges, I believe all of us are better served. My hope is that this book will empower women lawyers to bring their whole selves to their work, to their loved ones, and to their lives.

Finally, each Lesson in this book is a unique expression from the contributor. Each woman is sharing her personal truth. She is not speaking for her law firm or employer.

Lesson 1

● ● ● ●

STAY CURIOUS
IDA ABBOTT

Curiosity has its own reason for existing. One cannot help but be in awe when he contemplates the mysteries of eternity, of life, of the marvelous structure of reality. It is enough if one tries merely to comprehend a little of this mystery every day.

— *ALBERT EINSTEIN*

Being a lawyer is tough. Working with lawyers is also tough, even when you're trying to help them. Yet after more than four decades as a lawyer and consultant in the legal profession, I still love what I do. One of the reasons for this long-term satisfaction is my abiding curiosity. There is so much I don't know, and every situation and person I encounter presents a chance to learn something new. Even if what I learn is of no particular significance, the experience is usually fun, useful, or even inspiring.

As children, we all start out curious. Every day is magical as we explore, inquire, and learn about everyone and everything that surrounds us. Many people, especially those who later become lawyers, continue that quest as we grow up. We love to learn, and we develop and pursue many interests. Then, as our careers take hold, much of that curiosity dims. We stop being inquisitive except as to work matters, especially when work pressures consume the time we'd like for other things. We become concerned about being seen as expert and professional, so we focus on answering, not asking questions. And because we worry about being perceived as anything less than an authority, we don't ask about things that might make us seem naive or uninformed. In the process, we lose the magic of exploration, inquiry and letting our minds run free. We also lose the sense of wonder that brings us joy.

Curiosity is marked by wanting to know more. It is motivated by a desire for new and challenging ideas and experiences. And its benefits are numerous.

Curiosity makes you a lifelong learner. It allows you to indulge your love of learning in countless directions. It can propel you to dig deeper into a subject that fascinates you, to learn a little about a lot of different things, and to explore far beyond your boundaries. It makes you a keen observer who finds new meaning in a familiar experience or is drawn to unusual subjects that pique your interest.

Curiosity is the driver of creativity. It moves you to search for fresh approaches and different ways of thinking and doing. When you ask "why" or "what if" instead of accepting things as they are, you are led toward new ideas, new solutions, and new possibilities in your work, career, and life.

Curiosity builds your resilience. It energizes you and keeps you from growing complacent or stale. Instead of succumbing to routine, your mind stays more active and engaged both at work and with the world. When things go badly or you're feeling down, you can recover more readily when you have other interests that divert you and give you pleasure.

Curiosity transforms ignorance or fear into an asset. We often feel afraid when we are in an unfamiliar situation, among strangers or people more expert than we are, or when we don't know what to say or expect from others. Not long ago, I helped develop a mentoring program for lawyers in a Middle Eastern country. I was confident in my knowledge of the subject matter, but everything else about the project was foreign to me, including the language, culture, and legal system. Rather than fret about my ignorance and "otherness," I used my curiosity to build rapport and trust. From our first meeting, I told the participants about myself, what I knew and what I didn't know, and I asked them to educate me while I helped them. As our work proceeded, we all learned a great deal from each other, and not just about mentoring.

Being curious makes you a better networker. Many (maybe most) lawyers resist networking. But having a strong network of personal and business relationships makes your life and career much easier. When you need to find an expert, a new job, or a babysitter, a strong network means you have people to call on for help. And curiosity can make networking painless, interesting, and even enjoyable. Almost everyone has something intriguing in their life, their work, or their past. When I meet someone new, I try to discover what it is. Personal stories often lead to enthralling conversations; business stories can produce reasons for meeting again. Both can lead to a deeper personal or business relationship. The key, though, is to be curious about what you can learn from or about the other person.

Curiosity makes you interesting to others. When you ask people about themselves and show a genuine interest, most people are pleased; many are flattered. Rather than think less of you or consider you uninformed, people appreciate that you're interested in what they do or know about.

Being curious makes you a better rainmaker. Connecting with people is essential to rainmaking. Building strong relationships – developing your social capital – increases the possibilities that business will come your way. Asking potential clients about their business and legal needs shows them you want to understand them and how you can best help them. Early in my consulting practice, I wrote columns on best practices in professional development for a new legal journal. Each column highlighted two or three firms engaged in that practice. As I interviewed those firms in depth, I learned not just their effective practices but also what their needs were. Researching those columns helped me build my expertise and reputation, and many of the firms I featured became clients.

Curiosity makes you a better lawyer. When you are curious about and interested in what you are doing, you tend to put in extra effort and do a better job. Intellectual curiosity enhances your knowledge of the law. Learning more about your clients, their motivations, and their predicaments expands your empathy and improves your ability to advise and represent them. Learning about the opposing parties and counsel improves your ability to create better strategies and achieve better solutions.

Perhaps most importantly, curiosity makes you a happier person. It opens windows to the unexpected and the wondrous. Your life is enriched when you pursue interests in the world around you, not just within the sphere of your job or the law. A narrow focus on tasks and routine closes you off to diversions and adventures that could bring you pleasure or excitement. When you are receptive to the unfamiliar, you are more likely to come upon opportunities to experience discovery, joy, and delight. A mindset and attitude that embrace novelty, even if just occasionally, can give rise to moments of insight, meaning, and happiness.

Ida Abbott is the president of Ida Abbott Consulting. Ida promotes and supports career development and advancement from the beginning of a lawyer's career through retirement. Ida has long been a leader in the field of talent management, particularly mentoring, leadership, and sponsorship, and she is co-founder of the Hastings Leadership Academy for Women and the Professional Development Consortium. She is a popular speaker and prolific author. She is also an elected fellow of both the American Bar Foundation and the College of Law Practice Management. Learn more about Ida at www.IdaAbbott.com.

Lesson 2

● ● ● ●

SHAPING YOUR OWN PATH TO CAREER SUCCESS, SATISFACTION, AND HAPPINESS

HEIDI S. ALEXANDER

Always remember to smell the flowers as you proceed along your life's path.

— *JUSTICE JAYNEE LAVECCHIA*

When I was 18 years old, I moved from a small town in Minnesota to attend an East Coast liberal arts college. At the end of those four years, I graduated with a fire inside of me, ambitious and motivated to change the world. I spent a few years volunteering for a variety of progressive causes as well as working full-time for a nonprofit women's business assistance center that helped minority and economically disadvantaged women start and grow businesses. I knew I was bound for a graduate degree in the future; indeed, many of my college classmates had already begun working toward their graduate degrees or even completed one. At that time, law school seemed to provide the most versatility (either there wasn't much talk about debt post-graduation, or I actively ignored it), even though the thought of actually practicing law also did not appeal per se. I figured, based on my interest in public service, politics, and policy, law school made the most sense for my future career prospects.

I attended a state school, Rutgers School of Law in Newark, New Jersey. I made the most of my law school experience—I led student-run activist groups, participated in a domestic violence survivor advocacy program, worked in the constitutional litigation clinic, served as editor-in-chief of the law review, and more. Upon graduation, I clerked for a justice on the highest court of the state of New Jersey. If that wasn't enough, at the same time I got my EMT license and volunteered on a local squad. After failed attempts to obtain a post-clerkship public interest fellowship, I focused my job search on joining a practice aligned with my passion to advance civil rights and to make a real difference in the world. After what felt like a never-ending spiderweb of networking, I stumbled upon a small general practice firm in Boston that excelled in special education and plaintiff's-side employment law. I joined as an associate with its employment law and litigation team.

This seemed like the right step for me. I would advocate for those who had been discriminated against in the workplace; I would contribute to amicus briefs on behalf of progressive organizations and causes; and I would have the opportunity to work with like-minded lawyers. What I didn't take into consideration was whether I'd actually enjoy the work. Clerking was a wonderful experience and taught me valuable skills, but I wasn't particularly good at it, nor did I love the actual work—reviewing loads of documents, conducting research, developing arguments, drafting memos, briefs, and even opinions. Yes, I said it. Feels nice to get that off my chest. If you are a litigator, then what I described to you might sound familiar. That's precisely what I was required to do as a young associate in an employment litigation practice. Who knew? Maybe I would have if I had stopped for a moment to identify my strengths, weaknesses, likes, and dislikes, instead being hyper-focused on some distant career vision. The idea of who I should be and what that meant for my career blinded me, and I was miserable because of it.

When I completed my clerkship year, the justice gave me a framed picture she had taken of a gorgeous flower. Under it, she wrote: "For Heidi, Always remember to smell the flowers as you proceed along your life's path." – Justice Jaynee LaVecchia 2010." And, she was right. That's precisely what I had failed to do.

Soon, I left the small law firm. I had neither jobs lined up nor any idea what I would do with my career. I spent the next few months engaged in self-exploration. I focused on things I liked to do. Things that made me happy. I experimented with organic farming, even drafting a business plan for my own small farm. Within a few months, I was running my consulting business working with law firms on their marketing and technology needs. I was making presentations at bar associations and networking with attorneys.

And, just like that, a job I didn't even know existed fell right in my lap. I was asked to interview as a practice management consultant for the Law Office Management Assistance Program, a program of Lawyers Concerned for Lawyers (LCL), our state's nonprofit lawyer assistance program. The stars aligned. It's been six years since I started working for LCL. I'm now the deputy director of the organization. Each day is rewarding, helping attorneys handle the stress of practice, keep apace with changes in the practice of law, and remain healthy both personally and professionally. Furthermore, I love the work. It can be technical, strategic, emotional, and personal. What's more is that I have balance. I've learned to handle stress in a positive way and to make time for my family.

If I had not "stopped to smell the flowers," I don't know where I'd be. I think many lawyers fall into this trap. For a number of reasons – debt, competition, tradition – law schools tend to feed students into large firms without providing other potential career options. But, not everyone fits that mold. If you find yourself somewhere that doesn't seem like the right fit, the thought of leaving will be scary and difficult. For me, it was one of the most challenging experiences of my life. I felt like I was giving up—that's not me; I'm full of ambition; I don't quit. But, sometimes quitting puts things into perspective. And, it's OK. I'm here to tell you that. There is always another job. The road there might not be easy, but I can promise you that another path exists.

Part of the reason I found the courage to leave and follow my heart (not my head) was because of a supportive partner and community. It's important to build a supportive community. These people might be family, friends, or other professionals. I discovered that not only were people willing to support me on my journey, but they wanted to help. One of my first clients in my consulting practice was a woman I had met at a bar association event. We had much in common and kept in touch. To this day, I continue to consult with her on practice management through my job. I'm now active in the Women's Bar Association and run a support group for other attorney moms ("Supermom"). These are all people who I consider part of my community.

Oftentimes, as attorneys, we are forced to put up a facade. We do it to appear confident and serve as the most effective advocate for our clients. This makes it even more difficult for us to let go and embrace change. Sometimes, removing that facade, as uncomfortable as it might be to dig deep inside, can produce remarkable results. It did for me. Just as the justice imparted to me, I encourage you to take a moment to "stop and smell the flowers." It may lead you to new experiences and opportunities, and even satisfaction in your life and career.

Heidi S. Alexander is the deputy director of Lawyers Concerned for Lawyers, where she helps manage organization operations and leads the Massachusetts Law Office Management Assistance Program (LOMAP). LOMAP provides free and confidential practice management assistance, guidance in implementing new law office technologies, and methods to attain healthy and sustainable practices. She is the author of *Evernote as a Law Practice Tool*, serves on the ABA's TECHSHOW Planning Board, and founded the ABA's Women of Legal Technology initiative. In 2017, Heidi was appointed to the Massachusetts Supreme Judicial Court's Standing Advisory Committee on Professionalism. She is a native Minnesotan, former collegiate ice hockey goaltender for the Amherst College women's ice hockey team, and mother of three young children. Learn more about Heidi at www.masslomap.org.

Lesson 3

●   ●   ●   ●

DISCOVERING YOUR AUTHENTIC SELF
SABRINA C. BEAVENS

*The only time you are really insecure or not sure of yourself is when
you are not being your authentic self.*

— *ROBIN ROBERTS*

She looked me in the eye and said, "You need to get comfortable in your
own skin." I doubt that she remembers saying it, but those words from my
mentor, Judge Pamela A. M. Campbell, struck me at my core. I recognize that
I was fortunate to receive her honest feedback, but it bothered me that she
called me out. I was a twenty-something new lawyer and had done very well
until that point. Why was Judge Campbell criticizing me? My self-perception
was that I projected as a very confident young attorney. After all, I had always
been a good student and excelled at most things that I tried, from athletics in
high school through the moot court board in law school. But my mentor saw
through all of that and called me on it.

Frankly, I was shocked that someone else could hear the voices in my
head. She called my bluff. She knew me well enough to know that I was struggling to be myself and that it would hold me back. Still, I did not take a lot of
time to reflect on her advice.

Several years later I watched Robin Roberts discuss being your authentic
self as a component of success on an episode of Good Morning America. I
remember hearing those words and feeling them resonate within me. I wrote
them on a sticky note. Perhaps for the first time, I gave greater thought to what
Judge Campbell said several years prior. I questioned whether I was being
authentic in both my career and personal life. I was not. This time I made a

conscious decision to change. But that change did not happen overnight. It was a process that involved the following:

Accepting my gifts. I am smart. I am a leader. I am funny. I am a good listener. I am someone who people trust. I have a big heart. However, these were not always natural gifts that I valued and at times, some gifts, such as being a leader, made me uncomfortable. I grew up long before Sheryl Sandberg proclaimed that "bossy" should be banned. I remember being called bossy at home and at school at an early age. As a result, I can recall situations where people looked at me to be a leader and feeling uncomfortable or shying away from that position. I have grown to accept and embrace these gifts—it is, after all, who I am. I have no problem being the center of attention and telling a good story to a group—I relish it! If someone needs to step up in a certain situation, I raise my hand. I have the shoulders that can carry the load and hopefully do the job. If someone needs an ear to listen, I am comfortable lending that ear. I have a big heart, and that does not make me weak. As I read this paragraph, it seems silly to me now that I felt like these qualities were not gifts.

Accepting who I love. The first draft of this lesson did not include a discussion about accepting myself as a gay woman. But if I am being authentic in my advice to you, this was as big of a step for me as accepting my gifts—perhaps bigger. I started law school in 1997 and met my wife around the same time. I would like to say that today is a much different time for a young gay attorney, but recent events have caused me to rethink that conclusion. As a young attorney getting to know members of the legal community, small talk often involves discussion about your family. I played the game of speaking in generalities or avoiding the topic altogether. That often resulted in one-sided conversations or awkward moments where I knew someone suspected that I was gay, but didn't ask. This was exhausting. It felt disrespectful to my wife to hide her existence and our happiness. Keeping the secret made me feel bad about myself.

I am so proud of my marriage and our family. I love them more than I can put into words. I grew my confidence over time and started engaging in conversations about my personal life rather than avoiding the topic. Being comfortable took practice. It was hard to speak honestly to people that I perceived may have moral or religious objections to being gay. But, I was tired of protecting their feelings and sacrificing my own. Being authentic about who I love and who I am was worth the risk of possibly offending a few people.

Accepting that not everyone will like me. Wanting to please and be liked by everyone are issues I think many of us struggle with, and we adapt our behavior accordingly. As attorneys, we are constantly introduced to new relationships through clients and as a part of marketing our business. The goal of marketing relationships, of course, is to be hired for new work. I accept that some prospective clients may choose not to hire me for any number of reasons. I'm OK with that. Or perhaps I hold a minority opinion in a group. Will that make the others not like me? Maybe. But if I try to be someone other than myself, I am definitely not being authentic and in the long run, the relationship likely will not be a good fit.

At the end of 2016, I found myself interviewing again after working at the same firm for many years. I definitely approached interviewing differently than the younger me Judge Campbell counseled all those years ago. I had years of experience and a client base to offer this time around, but I was more confident when I interviewed because I was the authentic me. I no longer let self-doubt creep into my mind. I was open about the value I place on working in an environment that allows people to be themselves. I was not interested in jamming myself into a mold of what a firm created as a model attorney. As a result, I landed at a firm that is a great fit for me. I am not restrained and frustrated by trying to be what I think my firm or our clients might want me to be. Instead, I am myself, which I believe makes me a better attorney for our clients and a better colleague at the firm.

Accepting that I am not perfect. Authentic me makes mistakes. I now realize that being hard on yourself for a mistake is like sinking in quicksand. The negative thoughts you tell yourself keep you weighed down and the longer that state continues, the harder it is to get back on the horse. It is OK to take a moment and experience disappointment when something does not go your way. Having awareness that I am too hard on myself and moving on from that state of mind has been helpful in managing stress and having the confidence to take risks and seek new opportunities.

In preparing this Lesson, I asked myself, "How can I evaluate whether I truly am living an authentic life?" Then, I remembered an exercise I recently participated in at the end of a month's-long leadership training program. The exercise involved my classmates saying one-word descriptions describing me in a short period of time. I was surprised at how many of the words my classmates used to describe me mirrored what I know as my true self: funny, smart, intense, dedicated, kind, creative, storyteller, clever, and initiative. At the end of the exercise, I felt like they really got to know the real me—and I felt more connected to them as a result.

So, take it from me who took years to follow my mentor's advice: Make it your goal to be your authentic self and be comfortable in your own skin. You will be surprised at the ripple effect that this awareness and freedom brings to your life. You'll have the added confidence to take risks, pursue goals, and share your thoughts and ideas with others. And if you're like me, you'll find an increased sense of inner peace and better relationships. It sounds cliché, but it is true: Life is far too short to be someone other than your authentic self. Who are you?

Sabrina C. Beavens is an attorney at Upton & Hatfield, LLP located in Concord, New Hampshire. After over 16 years as an attorney in private practice, Sabrina has developed a reputation as a personable attorney who is well-versed in a wide range of practice areas.

After graduating law school in 2002, Sabrina worked as a bankruptcy and civil litigation attorney in Florida. In 2006, Sabrina relocated to New Hampshire, where she joined a small law firm in Dover. After a few years, Sabrina returned to her prior Florida firm and opened a satellite office in Portsmouth. For several years, she enjoyed a snowbird lifestyle representing clients in both Florida and New Hampshire. With the addition of her daughter to her family in 2013, Sabrina decided to focus on her New Hampshire practice and joined Upton & Hatfield. Currently, Sabrina spends most of her time working on transactional matters such as representation of small to midsize companies, banking and commercial transactions, real estate, and estate planning. However, she still enjoys helping clients with select litigation matters.

Sabrina is AV-rated by Martindale-Hubbell. She served as co-chair of the American Bar Association Section of Litigation Woman Advocate Committee where she also completed a Leadership Fellowship and received the Outstanding Subcommittee Chair Award. She has written numerous articles on legal and practice-related topics and presented at several seminars. Sabrina is a proud alumnus of Stetson University College of Law and Ursinus College. Learn more about Sabrina at www.uptonhatfield.com.

Lesson 4

● ● ● ●

DEVELOPING A BOOK OF BUSINESS
ASHLEY L. BELLEAU

The key to success is action, and the essential in action is perseverance.

— SUN YAT-SEN

Whether you call it networking, marketing, or developing a book of business, it is a must for a woman (or a man). Your destiny depends on it. As Melanie D. Wilson reported in her article, *Sentencing Inequality Versus Sentencing Injustice*, in the July 2014 issue of *The Federal Lawyer*, women lag behind men in pay for equal work and in positions of prestigious employment. The statistics are telling. One author has observed a trend of little to no increase of female CEOs, CFOs, and board members over the past three years, noting a particular absence of influential businesswomen in Fortune 500 companies. Others have lamented the lack of women in academic positions, representing only a quarter of university presidents and even fewer law school deans.

Law360 recently reported in its annual Glass Ceiling Report that women only account for 21 percent of equity partners and 12 percent of the highest firm leadership roles. Of roughly 350 law firms surveyed recently, only about 40 have a female lawyer in a top leadership role. The dearth of female representation in leadership roles means women have less of a say in firm direction and workplace policy. But promisingly, the data displays a link between success of younger female associates and firms with women in leadership roles. Therefore, to narrow the gap and to command both respect and equal pay, women need to have and control a book of business.

Rainmakers bring value to a law firm and firms take notice. A strong book of business allows you to move into firm management positions and possibly onto the compensation committee. It can also afford you the opportunity to change firms if desired and avoid being laid off when the firm downsizes or implodes. If a woman doesn't have a book of business, her career is in the hands of others. This Lesson addresses tips on how to develop your book of business and stay visible.

BUILDING RELATIONSHIPS

Early in your career, your first relationships are built within the firm. Your first clients are through mentors who have business. The key is to make yourself invaluable to those partners. Develop good legal skills and always be timely with projects.

The potential to inherit business from elder attorneys is there, but it is *not guaranteed*. Don't fall into the trap of, "If I just do good work, clients will come, or clients will stay." Today, attorneys switch firms and so do clients.

Develop relationships outside the firm. Find your passion! If you are a leader, get involved in young leadership programs. If you are altruistic, help the local art museum or provide *pro bono* services for a nonprofit. Volunteerism brings relationships! Get involved in the community, politics, the bar association, or your place of worship. These connections help to develop a book of business. Volunteering time to speak on legal topics or write articles can also bring business.

LEARN TO "TOOT YOUR OWN HORN WITHOUT BRAGGING."

In order to build relationships with potential new clients or referral sources, women need to develop conversational strategies. For many attorneys, their biggest marketing challenge is the ability to speak about what they do. Most attorneys aren't comfortable talking about themselves, what they do, and how they help others. There are simple ways to develop these skills.

One such strategy is storytelling. Men often are good storytellers. One of the most interesting books I have read and share with new associates is *BRAG! The Art of Tooting Your Own Horn Without Blowing It*. In her book, author Peggy Klaus provides several strategies and exercises to help you develop your "braggables" and tell meaningful, interesting short stories.

Stories can be used to deliver communication in a simple but powerful fashion. Telling a story about a recent case you worked on and won for the client can be an effective means of relationship building. Make it relatable to build a bond.

How do you explain what you do? Don't just say "I am a lawyer." This doesn't make you stand out. Take this opportunity to tell a story. If you are a construction lawyer, speak about new construction projects. If you are a litigator, speak about your clients' successes.

Consider your audience. Speak about estate planning to someone at your place of worship. Explain how you guided a client through a business contract to a business owner. Know your "war stories" and share them. Women build relationships and trust through stories.

PUT YOUR GAME FACE ON.

People are watching! Project confidence. Whether in the firm, in court, networking, or at a community event, remember who you represent. You represent yourself and your law firm 24/7!

Be cognizant of what you post on all social media platforms. Women are often held to a higher standard than their male counterparts. They are often expected to act "lady-like" at all times. Clients do not want to see their attorney taking selfies or partying at a local bar. Never post anything you would not want your grandmother to see on the front page of the newspaper or find on YouTube!

LEARN TO ASK FOR BUSINESS IN A PROFESSIONAL WAY.

Be direct and stay on-point. In my own experiences, female lawyers are expected to be diplomatic and polite, not direct. To earn business, women must learn to be direct in their approach to developing business. Direct and on-point requires preparation. Research a client or potential client's business, industry, and customer base. Don White, a consultant to law firms for new business development, says we need to get into the client's "95 percent zone." He means find out what is important to the prospect. Find out what keeps them up at night. Then, use the information to bring them peace of mind and minimize their potential exposure.

Always *ask* for the business and gain a meeting. Meet for breakfast or lunch – even coffee – to learn about the prospective client's business and issues, then clearly address their concerns and define how you can help.

ASK FOR ADVICE FROM YOUR "SPONSOR" IN THE FIRM ABOUT HOW TO DEVELOP BUSINESS.

"Sponsors" are attorneys who interviewed you and recommended you for the firm. As your sponsor, it's in their best interest to have you succeed.

In her article, *Women of Color in Legal Education: Challenging the Presumption of Incompetence*, Carmen González, Professor of Law at Seattle University of Law, explains that in addition to mentors, women need sponsors who will advocate for them in "faculty meetings and behind closed doors when they are being reviewed for tenure and promotion." Professor González reports part of the problem is that "senior faculty tend to choose protégées who look like themselves and to overlook newcomers who are perceived as 'different,'" sometimes known as the "cloning effect." It typically occurs during the hiring process. Women should use this knowledge to forge a bond with the sponsoring attorney and make them an ally.

Another ally is the firm marketing professional. If your firm has a marketing professional on staff, ask for help to prepare a business development and a personal marketing plan. If a marketing professional is not available, look to a firm rainmaker for advice on how to build a book of business.

Women have more opportunities and job security if they become rainmakers.

In summary, be "braggadocious" and control your destiny! In order to be successful, you've got to make marketing a habit.

In *BRAG!*, Peggy Klaus identifies 12 tips for bragging that will help you build relationships, develop your book of business and stay visible:

1. Be your best, authentic self.
2. Think about to whom you are tooting.
3. Say it with meaningful and entertaining stories.
4. Keep it short and simple.
5. Talk with me, not at me.
6. Be able to back up what you say.
7. Know when to toot.
8. Turn small talk into big talk.
9. Keep braggologues and brag bites current and fresh.
10. Be ready in a moment's notice.
11. Have a sense of humor.
12. Use it all: your eyes, ears, head, and heart.

Women should implement these tips to develop their own book of business, take control of their careers, and "stay visible." Avoid others controlling your career. Remember: Everything you do and say is a form of marketing. Embrace it. Enjoy it. And have fun developing business and building new relationships!

Ashley L. Belleau was named a Top 25 Women *Louisiana Super Lawyer for 2019* and a *Louisiana Super Lawyer* in the area of Business Litigation. She also was recognized by *Best Lawyers* 2019 and is a *Recognized Practitioner* by Chambers and Partners USA in its Commercial Litigation category. Ashley advises businesses and individuals concerning bankruptcies, contracts, construction, fidelity, surety, and financial institution bonds, insurance, professional malpractice, corporate law, and estate matters. Ashley also mediates and arbitrates business disputes.

As a business owner herself, first as the owner of a publishing company, and then an owner and managing partner of a law firm, she understands the need for efficiency in the management and marketing of a business and how to address the employee and financial aspects of a business.

Ashley serves on the board of directors of the law firm, Lugenbuhl, Wheaton, Peck, Rankin & Hubbard, in its New Orleans office. She has been recognized for her accomplishments by *New Orleans CityBusiness* which named her to the 2016 Class of Leadership in Law and 2012 Class of Women of the Year.

A native of Mobile, Alabama, Ashley received her B.A. from Newcomb College and her J.D. from Tulane University School of Law. Upon graduating from Tulane University School of Law, she clerked in the Eastern District of Louisiana for the late Judge Henry A. Mentz, Jr. and was awarded the Eastern District of Louisiana *Distinguished Service* Award. Learn more about Ashley at www.lawla.com.

Lesson 5

● ● ● ●

CHANCES & AMPERSANDS

NORA RIVA BERGMAN

I take my chances.
I don't mind working without a net.
I take my chances.
I take my chances every chance I get.

— MARY CHAPIN CARPENTER

Before I went to college and law school, I was a professional musician. I played the guitar and sang. Still do—sometimes. Music has always been a big part of my life. In fact, my first TV memory was watching the Beatles on the Ed Sullivan Show. I was only four years old, but after the show, I nagged my dad until he bought me the "Meet the Beatles!" album. I still have it. When I was a kid, all I wanted to do was listen to music and learn to play the guitar. I could never have imagined where my life would take me. From growing up in Wilton Manors, Florida, to becoming a musician – yes, I did learn to play the guitar – to going to law school, practicing law, teaching, running a bar association, coaching other lawyers, and now having the privilege of writing a book with 49 incredible women as contributors.

This life is one awesome journey. The thing about journeys is…they can be risky. You might not be sure of the best route to take to get to your destination. Sometimes you might not even be sure of your destination. And you know what? That's OK.

When I was growing up, becoming a lawyer was not something I ever imagined doing. In fact, it was probably the furthest thing possible from what I wanted to do. I wanted to play music. I wanted to write songs. I did that for nearly 10 years after I graduated from high school. Then I realized I wanted something more. I didn't know what it was, but I knew it was something different from what I was doing. So, I took a chance.

After 10 years out of school, I decided it was time for me to go back. And it was very scary. I never thought of myself as a great student, and I hadn't been in a classroom for 10 years. I was 10 years older than most of my class-mates. I felt more of a kinship with some of my professors than with the other students. And I didn't know what I wanted to do when I got out of college. I decided to work toward a journalism degree. I liked to write songs; maybe that would translate to other kinds of writing. As part of my major, I had to take a class in First Amendment Law. That class was fascinating. I loved it. So, I took another chance.

I decided to apply to law school. But I was in my late 20s, and I was concerned about how old I'd be when I graduated. I remember talking to one of my journalism professors and saying, "If I go to law school, I'll be 32 when I graduate!" Her response, "How old will you be in four years if you don't go to law school?" So, I took the LSAT and did pretty well. Then, I took another chance.

I applied to only one law school. Stetson University College of Law had a wonderful reputation, was highly ranked, and was in my backyard—figura-tively speaking. I had no intention of moving to go to law school. If law school was meant to be, it was going to be Stetson. It was Stetson. I'm not sure what I expected, but I will tell you that every day of my first semester at Stetson I wanted to drop out. Every day I would go to the library and say to myself, "OK, if you can get through today, then you can think about dropping out tomorrow." Something about it just didn't feel right for me. Yet at the same time, I was beginning to like it. The first semester went by, then another semester, and another. I was still alive. I worked hard and got on law review. Then in what seemed like the blink of an eye, it was graduation day.

Graduating from law school in 1992 was a bit of a challenge. The country was still in a recession, and law firms were not hiring. The firm I had clerked for during law school had no positions available. I didn't want to work for a big firm. I didn't even want to interview with a big firm. I knew big firm life wasn't for me. I took another chance.

I decided to put myself to work. The firm I clerked for during law school had me working on civil rights and discrimination matters during that time. I loved this area of law, so I continued to do contract work for them and other firms. I started to build my own practice. I met an incredible attorney who is one of my closest friends to this day. This time it was she who took the chance—on me. We started a law firm. We took a chance.

My partner was board certified in workers' compensation law; I focused on employment discrimination law representing employees. It was a great fit. Another attorney and friend mentored me in federal practice. I had my first five-day federal jury trial with him. It was exhilarating and terrifying. It was a tremendous learning experience. We lost. But that trial helped me prepare for another. I was representing the first female firefighter hired by the City of Tampa. That case settled the night before jury selection. My client's story and the settlement reported in the news. She left her employment with the city, and she and her husband started a whole new life. They remain dear friends to this day.

Those two cases taught me a lot about myself. I learned that I didn't enjoy litigation. I knew that I was fighting for good people, and I could put on the battle gear each day. But I didn't like it. It wasn't me. Not long after, I lived through an ampersand. My mom and aunt were both killed in an automobile accident. With an ampersand, there is a before & after. That day was an ampersand in my life. Before the accident & after. I realized that when I left home in the morning there was no guarantee that I was coming back. This ampersand made it crystal clear that I had to make change. You guessed it. I took another chance.

I left my law practice and my wonderful law partner to become the executive director of our local bar association. In that role, I found me. The real me. I loved the work. I loved our members. I loved my staff. I loved being able to help other lawyers improve their lives and their practices. That role led me to taking another chance – becoming a business coach for lawyers, and another – writing my first book, and now a second book. I know there are many chances yet to take.

My Lesson: Don't be afraid to take your chances. And pay attention to the ampersands in your life.

Nora Riva Bergman is a business coach and author. She is the founder of Real Life Practice and a certified Atticus Practice Advisor. A licensed attorney since 1992, she has practiced as an employment law attorney and certified mediator and has served as an adjunct professor at both Stetson University College of Law and the University of South Florida. Nora received her undergraduate degree in journalism, *summa cum laude*, from the University of South Florida and her J.D., *cum laude*, from Stetson University College of Law, where she was a member of the Stetson Law Review and served as a mentor for incoming students. Learn more about Nora at www.reallifepractice.com.

Lesson 6

* * * *

YOU DECIDE WHAT IT MEANS TO BE SUCCESSFUL

NICOLE BLACK

There's only one thing to do at a moment like this...strut.

— *BART SIMPSON*

Everyone wants to be a "success." But what does that mean, and who decides what constitutes success? The answer isn't as complicated as it might seem. You define success, no one else.

It is so important for young attorneys – especially women – to acknowledge and embrace this concept. Don't let anyone else define success for you. Allowing others to do so is a mistake and one that has the potential to drastically affect your sense of self-worth for years to come.

A DIFFICULT LESSON TO LEARN

This was a lesson I learned the hard way in 2003, when I left the law firm where I worked as an associate. I'd been there for nearly four years – after another four years working for the public defender's office – even though I'd never envisioned myself in a law firm. And yet there I was.

But, it wasn't the right fit for me. I wasn't happy. I felt trapped, claustrophobic. I couldn't put my finger on it, although I knew that work-life balance had something to do with it. But that wasn't the sole problem.

I had one child at that time and planned to have at least one more. Although I could litigate and procreate, I had the sneaking suspicion that something had to give—either the quality of my work or my marriage and family. And, assuming that I even had a choice, I wasn't willing to choose between one or the other.

But that wasn't the only issue. I also felt as if my creative side was dying a slow death, almost as if a part of my brain was shutting down. The law was suffocating me. I'd entered law school with a strong Type A personality to begin with, and Lady Law had warped it into something nearly unrecognizable and unbearable. I didn't like who I'd become. I wanted out.

CHANGING PRIORITIES

Also of import was that over time, I realized that starting a family had fundamentally altered my priorities—and my definition of success. Many of the internal conflicts that I felt during my pregnancy and in the years that followed were tremendously difficult. I wrestled with feelings of personal inadequacy and worried that I wouldn't be able to maintain the high professional standards that I expected of myself. I also worried that I would be incapable of both working and mothering my child in a way that would not render me an unfit parent.

But at the heart of it, what I ultimately determined was that it wasn't the practice of law that I had issues with—it was the way that I was practicing it.

So, my husband, a nurse, who had been the primary caregiver for our daughter, transitioned to full-time employment while I took some time off and tried to figure out where I wanted to go with my professional life.

During this brief hiatus from the legal field, I experienced extreme guilt. I felt as if I had single-handedly derailed the entire feminist movement and failed women lawyers everywhere. In retrospect, I clearly gave myself far too much credit!

That being said, I wish I had known then what I know now: Success is a fluid, and very personal, concept. Had I known that then, I'd have spared myself a lot of unnecessary angst.

REIMAGINING SUCCESS

After a few years, I realized that I needed to return to law on my own terms. I missed logical thinking and legal writing. So, nearly three years after I'd left the law, I re-entered it. In 2005, I hung a virtual shingle as a contract attorney and simultaneously started blogging. And now, 13 years later, I've found a path that works for me. I've been employed as a "legal technology evangelist" for six years by MyCase, a company that provides legal practice management software for solo lawyers and small firms. I'm also an author, a legal technology journalist, and I speak often at venues across the country about the intersection of law and technology.

In other words, I successfully re-entered the legal space and reshaped my destiny, something I wasn't sure was even possible when I left my position at my old firm in 2003.

Here's the good news: It was possible. Now don't get me wrong. I realize that the law can be all encompassing. It's always been that way, hence the saying "the law is a jealous mistress." And attempting to balance one's chosen career with other non-legal obligations such as the demands of family life can be a delicate and difficult task for both male and female lawyers.

The problem is that many young lawyers are afraid to alter their course, even though they're incredibly unhappy, because they're afraid that doing so indicates that they've failed. Others are afraid that once off the ladder, they'll never be able to get back on. Rest assured, that's not the case.

DARE TO CREATE YOUR OWN PATH

A while ago I was reading a magazine, and in it was a section that focused on working mothers that consisted of interviews with a number of working women. In one of the interviews, an executive director of a hospital opined that she didn't judge women who left work after having a child. But then she added the one comment that strikes fear in the hearts of those who are considering leaving their current job: "(T)he hard thing is, 'How do you get back in?'"

How do you get back in? And what does that even mean "to get back in"? Is it as difficult as many would claim? Is your professional life over if you leave work when your children are young—smack dab in the middle of what some would claim is the most important part of your climb up the ladder to a "successful" career?

My answer—a resounding no. Your career is not over. Your legal career with that particular employer is probably over. And, you may have to redefine what "success" means to you. In particular, you'll have to ignore how other lawyers, especially those in law firms, define a "successful" legal career. But, you will be able to re-enter the workforce and have a successful and fulfilling career when you do decide to return to the working world.

YOU DEFINE "SUCCESS"

I read a study a few years back that suggested that professionals who have left the workforce to care for their children should try to return to the workforce within three years, at least on a part-time basis. The reason given for that recommendation was twofold: Employers tend to believe that you've been out of the loop for too long after more than a three-year break; and more importantly, you face a psychological barrier after three years that prevents you from believing that you can do it.

So, keep that three-year marker in mind. And, don't listen to those who say you can't "get back in." You can. It'll take some creativity and ingenuity. You'll have to think outside the box. And, you'll have to network. But you can do it. And, you will. And, you'll succeed—on your own terms.

In other words, you need to define success for yourself and understand that your concept of success must be flexible, since both time and your frame of reference tend to alter your vision of success. If you buy into someone else's concept of "success," you are bound to be miserable.

The bottom line: Success is in the eye of the beholder. Never let anyone else define success for you. That's a determination that you – and you alone – should make.

Nicole Black is a Rochester, New York attorney, author, journalist, and the legal technology evangelist at MyCase, legal practice management software. She is the nationally recognized author of *Cloud Computing for Lawyers* (2012) and co-authored *Social Media for Lawyers: The Next Frontier* (2010), both published by the American Bar Association. She also co-authored *Criminal Law in New York*, a Thomson West treatise. She writes regular columns for the *ABA Journal, the Daily Record, Above the Law,* and *Legal IT Pros,* has authored hundreds of articles for other publications, and regularly speaks at conferences regarding the intersection of law, mobile and cloud computing, and internet-based technology. Learn more about Nicole at www.mycase.com.

Lesson 7

● ● ● ●

DON'T LISTEN TO YOUR FATHER: HOW IGNORING THE WELL-INTENTIONED CAN MAKE YOU WEALTHY

ELIZABETH R. BLANDON

Nobody can give you wiser advice than yourself.

— MARCUS TULLIUS CICERO

If prayer is focusing on an idea with a firm belief that it will become reality, my father and I were both atheists who prayed. That is all we had in common. He was born on a backwoods farm in Cuba the year the world's economy hit rock bottom. I was born in New York in 1969, the year the internet was invented.

He focused on the myriad disasters that could befall his loved ones. In short, he worried incessantly. Go to California? Are you kidding—with those fault lines? His past experiences included surviving the Great Depression and fleeing his homeland. I understand why he lacked rose-colored glasses. To the opposite extreme, I focus unfailingly on bringing irrational goals to fruition. I dream with eyes open of a future where nothing is impossible. Don't you see, the word *impossible* says *I'm Possible*? This hope was born in the incredible events of my generation: the moon landing, the Civil Rights Act, and the proliferation of smartphones.

Thinking back on our relationship, I know he loved me. Just as strongly, however, I know that discounting his guidance, as highlighted below, led to my professional success.

"I AM TOO BUSY."

I remember that my parents, my brother, and I ate dinner together every night. We watched Wild Kingdom on Sundays. During the week, after finishing homework, I would sit on the living room couch devouring library books, while my father reviewed endless heaps of business documents. The stacks seemed to compete with me, growing two inches for every inch of mine.

We did not vacation outside Florida. My father did not play with me. He did not teach me to ride a bicycle or to roller skate. For these requests, his answer was, "I am too busy." As a child, I was initially impressed that his business was so important. As an adult, I realize that statement is shorthand for "You are not a priority."

Despite my career, my networking, my friends, and my hobbies, I never say "I am too busy." Even when I'm pulling my hair out. Even when I'm pressing my foot on the accelerator to get to an appointment. There will never be a lack of obligations. Being successful requires doing only what is important. For everything else, courageously admit that it is not a priority.

"YOU HAVE TO TAKE ALL CLIENTS."

Immigrants often work several jobs. My father was no exception. At different points in his life, he sold office supplies, price label machines, and pots and pans. No surprise, then, that when I opened my law firm in 2002, he thought I should not specialize in a particular area of law. This is a common misconception. Becoming an expert in a specific field makes it easier to dominate your market. I am the former chairperson of political asylum cases for the South Florida chapter of the American Immigration Lawyers Association. We represent clients throughout the U.S.

"MAKING MONEY IS HARD."

Years pass quickly. My firm is now 16 years old and my daughters are responsible young ladies. After my father retired, I visited him on weekends. We attempted the civil conversations we never had in my youth. He seemed confused when I said business was good and work was fun. But it can be and – given that we are playing in this theater called Earth only for a limited release – work should be fun.

Any successful lawyer owes an enormous debt of gratitude to his or her team. Defending the employees who save my clients' lives is my number-one responsibility. I hire people who will improve the collegial environment, who are problem solvers, and who run the firm during the many times when I cannot. Marketing lunches, business development seminars, and vacations… woo-hoo, baby, bring it on.

"DON'T TELL ANYONE HOW MUCH MONEY YOU MAKE."

I never knew my father's yearly income. Not even when I started managing his finances after he lost part of his vision. He was an extremely private man. Out of respect, I twisted myself into a pretzel to avoid knowing specific numbers. Humility was part of it. He equated speaking about finances with bragging.

I neither boast nor hide. My law firm's monthly income is written in large black marker on a whiteboard in the kitchen. Team members receive bonuses based on it so, yes, everyone knows how much coin comes in. "What you appreciate appreciates," author Jen Sincero wrote. I simply cannot imagine becoming a wealthy owner of a law firm without focusing laser beam attention on the numbers.

"DON'T TELL ANYONE YOUR POLITICS."

Inside my home, my father raged at the radio over the politics of his island nation and raged at the television over the incompetence of several U.S. presidents. Outside our home, however, he never spoke about politics. He never volunteered nor attended a march. And, though I remember standing beside him many times as he tried to sell this widget or that gizmo, I cannot recall him sharing any opinion on any issue with any client.

My politics are well known. Before the candidates took the stage at the only 2016 Democratic Presidential Debate in Florida, I spoke about immigration. Blandon Law is a citizen-creating machine and voting is the highest privilege of citizenship. Choosing what policies our society should follow and who we trust to make those policies a reality…that's high-level stuff. I agree with Dr. Seuss: "Those who matter don't mind and those who mind, don't matter."

The year before my speech at the Presidential Debate, my father became very ill. My brother and mother were there, but – as it happened – I was the only one by his bedside when he took his last breath in March 2015. I did not have the chance to tell him that in 2017 I was invited to discuss my invention, the Case Concierge, at a summit of some of the country's most entrepreneurial attorneys. Probably for the best. He would have replied, **"Don't tell anyone your ideas."**

Well, Dad, I'm writing my ideas about how to become wealthy. It's going to be published…

Elizabeth R. Blandon is the founder of Blandon Law, a Weston, Florida-based firm specializing in immigration, naturalization, and consular law matters for foreign nationals worldwide. Board certified by The Florida Bar in Immigration & Nationality Law, Elizabeth is the recipient of the Broward County Hispanic Bar Association's *Bravo! Award* for her leadership in public service, and the Broward County Bar Association's *2017 Section Chair Award* for her numerous educational seminars and volunteer activities.

Elizabeth currently serves as chairperson of the Immigration & Nationality Law Board Certification Committee for The Florida Bar and of the Immigration Section for the Broward County Bar Association. She has also been appointed as chair of the Asylum Committee for the South Florida Chapter of the American Immigration Lawyers Association.

Fluent in English, French, and Spanish, Elizabeth has assisted foreign nationals from over 80 countries and all 50 states. She is an advocate for victims of domestic violence and a tireless champion for those seeking asylum in the United States. Learn more about Elizabeth at www.asylum-abuse-immigration-lawyer.com

Lesson 8

● ● ● ●

FIND A MENTOR – BE A MENTOR
SANDRA BROWN

A mentor is someone who allows you to see the hope inside yourself.

— OPRAH WINFREY

According to Dictionary.com, a mentor is "a wise and trusted counselor or teacher" and "an influential senior sponsor or supporter." All of my early mentors were men. My law school mentor, and all of the attorneys who trained me in the area of entertainment law were men. I am thankful for all of them because I received excellent training; but I think it would have been helpful to have had a woman or a minority woman attorney as a mentor as I made early career decisions.

WOMEN LAWYERS ENTERING THE PROFESSION NEED MENTORS.

Young women lawyers are high achievers. They have graduated from high school, attended college, gotten into and graduated from law school, passed the bar, and started a very strenuous career. But, they are sometimes frustrated – as I was – with how difficult it is to find a mentor.

My advice to young women lawyers is: Don't become angry or frustrated, because 10-20 years from now, the person who does not have the time to sit and chat with a young lawyer could be *you*. It's not that established women lawyers don't have the desire to provide advice; it's just that there may not be any more hours left in the day to spend speaking with or teaching a young lawyer without compromising one's own physical well-being.

So, how does a young lawyer go about finding a mentor? You can start by reaching out to potential mentors within your law school alumnae association—preferably before you graduate. After graduating from law school, there are a number of options you can explore.

- State bar organizations. Your mentor does not need to be in your practice area, but it is helpful.
- Potential mentors within your firm, practice group, or law department.
- Women attorneys in other firms, companies, or business organizations.
- Conferences. Your first choice would be to find an attorney in the city where you live and work because it makes it easier to get together for breakfast, lunch, or coffee, and to stay in touch. But, if you meet an attorney at a national conference, make the extra effort to try to stay in touch.
- Cultural organizations. There may be a strong community behind one's heritage that should not be overlooked. Community ties or cultural ties may later play a role in your career as resources for business development or leads to employment opportunities.

MINORITY WOMEN LAWYERS

When I was in law school, I read an article about an African-American woman attorney transitioning from a big firm in Los Angeles to head Warner Bros. Records. I had reservations about entering the practice area of entertainment law because until reading that article, I hadn't found any minority women in entertainment law in my research. Once I became a lawyer, and after joining the Black Entertainment and Sports Law Association (BESLA), I had the pleasure of meeting a founding member of the organization and first woman African-American entertainment attorney. As I became more established in my career, I was exposed to other African-American women with excellent credentials who had succeeded professionally, holding titles like senior VP, office of the chairman & CEO at Warner/Chappell Music. There were only a few, but they were influential in motivating me in a predominantly male culture.

There are more minority women lawyers in entertainment law (and other practice areas) today; but unfortunately biases still exist. The young minority women lawyers I have spoken with still find it difficult to get the early guidance required to advance to partner level in "BigLaw" or get promoted to senior counsel positions in-house. If you are a young minority woman lawyer not finding a mentor within your own firm or at your current place of employment, it is important that you find minority mentors outside your firm. It's helpful to have someone senior to discuss challenges you may be having, such as getting substantive work assignments, resume building, career moves, interviewing, offers, salaries, and even very personal decisions that impact long-term career goals, such as getting married and starting a family.

CAN PEERS OR NON-ATTORNEYS BE MENTORS?

My peers have been instrumental in my career. For example, one of my close non-attorney friends had some prior experience in the music industry and suggested early in my career that I should try to work for a music production company instead of just looking to work at law firms. I had no idea at that time that this was possible. That suggestion led to my first job as associate director of business affairs for So Def Recordings, Inc. and Artistic Control Management, Inc. and launched my career as an entertainment lawyer. I also had friends who went to BigLaw before I did, so each time I had the opportunity to transition to BigLaw, my peers helped me prepare for the process.

Family members and parents, even if they are not lawyers, can also act as ad hoc mentors and sometimes get overlooked. Parents who are not lawyers may still provide emotional support when you need to talk through career advancement challenges. Family members who may be in other professions, such as health care or accounting, may have thoughts for you, as they may have faced somewhat similar challenges in establishing their careers. Non-lawyer mentors are not a substitute for mentors who are lawyers, but they are valuable when taking into consideration the bigger picture for your career and your life as a whole.

SENIOR WOMEN LAWYERS SHOULD BE MENTORS.

Clients, spouse, children and their homework and extracurricular activities, boards/organizations, exercise, sleeping, caregiving, volunteer work, religious or other spiritual commitments...women lawyers manage all of it. But, because we have smartphones, voiceover IP phones, laptops, and tablets, we can work from virtually anywhere. We are no longer stuck behind our desks, so we have more time to do what we want to do, when we want to do it, right?

"Work-life balance" has become a trendy topic, but is anyone truly experiencing it yet? Today's working world is so "plugged in" and everyone believes that you should be more accessible than ever before. No, we are not stuck in the office behind a desk as much anymore, but we find ourselves working at the doctor's office, at the airport, or unfortunately, at kids' soccer games, basketball games, or swim meets, instead of being "present" in other important moments of our lives. We seem to have less free time because we are *always* working. And, now I am suggesting you add "mentoring" to your list.

There is mutual benefit to mentoring a young lawyer because even as senior attorneys, there is always a need to grow your network. Finding mentees requires very little effort at this point in a senior attorney's career, so you don't need to add it to the "to do" list. You cross paths with potential mentees probably more frequently than you realize. Just try to remain open. We were all new lawyers at one time. You've likely been where the young women around you currently are and have made it over the early career hurdles. We have all experienced similar desires, emotions, and anxieties. Sharing our prior experiences can be more helpful than you think. Helping another woman avoid certain pitfalls and move a little easier through her career can be professionally and personally rewarding and is a great contribution to our profession for years to come.

Sandra Brown is an entertainment attorney and partner with Taylor English Duma, LLP. Licensed in New York and Georgia, Sandra represented high-profile talent in her own entertainment law practice, prior to joining Taylor English. She has focused her career on working with award-winning talent. Motivated by the values of honor, integrity, and consummate legal knowledge, Sandra is dedicated to supporting and giving back to the entertainment and education community. Sandra started her legal career as the associate director of business affairs for the entertainment companies owned by hit music producer and now Reality TV Producer, Jermaine Dupri.

Prior to joining Taylor English, she advised clients generally in the areas of music and television. Her clients' musical credits included Usher, Mariah Carey, Janet Jackson, Michael Jackson, Alicia Keys, Mary J. Blige, Daughtry, Akon, Gwen Stefani, Eminem, and Lady Gaga. Sandra has also counseled professional athletes in various entertainment and business ventures as well. Before establishing her own practice, Sandra spent five years of counsel to the entertainment group of a large international law firm representing managers, entertainment television corporations, and numerous Grammy

Award–winning artists and producers in country, rock, pop, and hip hop. Sandra is a member of the National Academy of Recording Arts and Sciences (NARAS), and Black Entertainment and Sports Lawyers Association (BESLA), and enjoys guest speaking at colleges and universities, including her alma maters, Florida State University and Nova Southeastern University, where she has served as a donor and volunteer. Learn more about Sandra at www.taylorenglish.com.

Lesson 9

• • • •

WHO SAYS I CAN'T? WATCH ME!

KIMBERLY CAMPBELL

To hell with circumstances, I create opportunities.

— BRUCE LEE

Do you ever realize how much one decision can change your life? Sometimes, you cannot even imagine. I am a sitting circuit court judge for two counties in Florida with almost 1.4 million people. Twenty years ago, I moved from a town with a total population of less than 60,000. How did this happen? What was the catalyst? Was it luck, hard work, perseverance, stubbornness, or all of the above?

In 1997, I was bored. I had a job I enjoyed, was married to a wonderful man, we had a great home, I was close to family, and I was bored. Johnson City, Tennessee, is the town where I grew up. I was 28 years old and had never lived outside of a 20-mile radius. I had just graduated from Milligan College, a local college, with a bachelor's degree in business management. My immediate family was small with only my parents and my older sister. However, my extended family reached over 80 with aunts, uncles, and cousins. Everyone married, stayed close to home, and had more children, adding to the already growing family unit. In 1997, only two other cousins had graduated from college. I was bored. My first mentor was my immediate boss, who allowed me to take on more and more responsibility after my graduation. He eventually asked me, "What do you want to do when you grow up?" At the time, I honestly did not know. I knew friends were graduating from college with nursing degrees and business degrees, I knew friends were working at factory jobs and becoming stay-at-home parents. I also knew I did not want any of that. I decided to take the LSAT, which is the entrance exam necessary to attend law school. I filled out an application for Stetson University College of Law and planned for the LSAT.

In the fall of 1997, I drove to Florida with my current company for a meeting and took the LSAT. No one knew. My husband didn't know; my parents didn't know; my sister didn't know. I didn't want anyone to know because I wasn't sure exactly what I was going to do. The day before the exam, I developed a 102-degree temperature. The day of the exam, I barely remember, other than thinking, "Well, that was a wash." I flew home the next day. I already had plans to travel with my husband to Nashville to celebrate his birthday in February. Why Nashville? Because I knew from filling out an application for Stetson Law School, they were doing in-person interviews in Nashville in February 1998. We drove to Nashville, and while he recovered from a night out, I meet with the interview board for Stetson and put my best foot forward. I don't remember much about the interview either, other than still not anticipating being accepted.

I basically forgot about the interview until one day, I was walking from the mailbox, and I had received a letter from Stetson. I wasn't even nervous opening it because I didn't expect much. I was astonished to be holding in my hands an acceptance letter for the summer 1998 class at Stetson University College of Law in Gulfport, Florida. I walked back into my house; my husband was drinking coffee, and I gave him the letter and said, "I'm moving to Florida."

Thus, began an adventure. My husband was shocked, my family dismayed I was actually thinking about moving, and I was still hesitant. I resigned from my job on my 28th birthday. I made plans to move May 18, 1998. I would drive a moving truck down with my two cats and me. Plans were not solidified with my husband because he "wanted to see what happened" and one of us needed a job. The day I pulled out of my driveway was the hardest day of my life until that point. I was leaving everything I knew, everyone I knew, and the safety and security of the known. I was jumping into the unknown.

My first year of law school was the hardest year of my life. I wanted to quit so many times, but I had decided long ago, I don't start something I don't finish. I decided to attempt to transfer law schools to be closer to home. I talked about this with my then-husband who admitted, "Your dad and I sent you to Florida because we didn't think you could do it." Bear in mind, I come from an area where many women still believe the man is the final say.

I think when I heard that comment, I saw red. I wasn't upset. I wasn't sad. I was angry! That one comment was the determining factor in my decision to stay in Florida and not only finish what I started, but to excel at it. That was the beginning of taking circumstances and making my own opportunities.

I was sworn into The Florida Bar two days after 9/11. For the next 12 years, I was an assistant state attorney, a private criminal defense and family law attorney, and a guardian ad litem for my judicial circuit. In 2012, I ran a successful campaign for circuit court judge, again because I was bored with the practice of law.

Twenty years after I took that leap into the unknown, I have more than I ever dreamt of. I have a life that a small-town girl from Johnson City didn't even imagine in 1998. I have a husband who is in the same field as I am, and who "gets" me and understands me; a son more precious to me than life itself; a family of in-laws who love me and accept me as one of their own, and are supportive and amazing; a house full of kitty cats who keep me laughing; a best friend who is more like a brother to me; more friends than I have ever had, many of whom are closer to me than family; and a career and future I love!

This is not to say the last 20 years have been easy. They haven't. I was diagnosed with breast cancer when I was 39, before my son was two years old. With wonderful doctors and fantastic friends, I came out even stronger. I've lost friends and loved ones and I've realized many people, family included, just seem to drift away. I've failed at many things, but I've used those failures to create more opportunities. It's been very hard, but the good always outweighs the bad. I am now reaping the benefits of a whim I took 20 years ago.

I started a bucket list when I turned 30 years old, all to be complete before I turned 50. That list is: 1) Be licensed to practice law – check; 2) Earn my black belt in martial arts – check; 3) Learn to scuba – check; 4) Go skydiving – check; 5) Travel to Europe – check; 6) Earn my pilot's license. The only one left "unchecked" is number 6, but I still have two years to complete that!

Failures create opportunities. Opportunities create change. Change creates strength. Strength creates an amazing woman. Be amazing.

Circuit Court Judge Kimberly Campbell grew up in Northeast Tennessee. She graduated from Stetson University College of Law with both a law degree and an MBA. She has worked as an assistant state attorney, a family law attorney and criminal defense attorney, as well as acting as a guardian ad litem. She has also served as a special magistrate for the Pinellas County

Construction Licensing Board. She has served as an adjunct professor with St. Petersburg College since 2008. In 2012, she was elected circuit court judge. In addition to her service on the court, Judge Campbell also serves on numerous boards. She served as president of the Clearwater Bar Association and is a member of Leadership Pinellas, the Clearwater Bar Foundation, the Pinellas Park Chamber of Commerce, and the National Alliance on Mental Illness. Judge Campbell is active in her son's activities and was the only female coach of his Palm Harbor Little League team.

Lesson 10

● ● ● ●

THEY WILL CRUSH YOU, IF YOU LET THEM. DON'T.

MARIA-VITTORIA "GIUGI" CARMINATI

I'm tough, I'm ambitious, and I know exactly what I want.
If that makes me a bitch, okay.

— MADONNA

As a young associate at large law firm, I worked hard. I arrived before everyone else and left after everyone else. I never spent less than 10 hours at the office on weekdays and always worked a few extra hours in the evening, after my son (and then children) went to bed. I traveled whenever requested. I made out-of-the-office engagements as brief as possible. I responded to emails immediately, regardless of the time of day. I dutifully did what I was told, regardless of the toll it took on me or my family. I tried to complete every task as fast as possible and as well as possible. I had one son during law school, another 19 months later, and another 23 months after that. I didn't skip a beat. I put my job before anything else. It wasn't enough.

At one review I was told I gave the impression of "not taking the job seriously." I was gutted. I was giving this job my all, scheduling my personal life down to the minute to make everything fit. While I was pregnant with my second son, a female partner gave me the best advice I didn't take. She said when it came to maternity leave, I should take all of it because nobody would remember I came back early—but everyone would remember if I struggled. I didn't listen; I thought doing more would be better. Instead of taking advantage of my full leave, I came back five weeks early. Nobody cared about my forfeited five weeks, but I was getting crushed by the work. I was also regularly reprimanded for being too direct with the staff. Eventually, the running joke became that I "communicated like a man." At one review, someone suggested I be "more feminine." They meant more submissive to the staff. Adding to this, my attitude that no job was too little or outside my duties earned me the reputation for being "an excellent paralegal." These two last statements were illustrative of the way I was viewed. No matter how hard I worked, something would always be "off." I eventually left the firm and started at a boutique.

They loved me there. How could they not? I was the engine on the biggest case they had. I worked 60 to 70 hours every week. I traveled incessantly. I worked every evening, every weekend, and most holidays. For two years, I made the firm money and pushed myself to the breaking point. In return, I wasn't getting paid enough, and when I asked for more resources and support, my requests were denied. Some nights I was so tired I would throw up while driving home. I woke up every day at 5:00 a.m. and regularly didn't go to bed until midnight or later. I eventually developed heart palpitations. I had a full workup and the cardiologist explained it was stress-related, would never resolve, and I needed to be on lifelong medication. For a person who ran five kilometers seven days a week, this was a devastating heartache—literally. (The heart condition did go away as soon as I stopped relying on one particular paralegal who made my life hell. At that point, my heart rate went back to normal—though I had to do all of her work as well as mine to get things done.)

When I traveled, I took off and landed at the crack of dawn or in the middle of the night. I would pour myself into an Uber and fall asleep instantly, waking up at home and dragging myself to bed only to start up again the next day. Because I wasn't getting paid enough, I took on translation jobs to make a little extra cash. My husband was in training, so I was effectively the sole breadwinner. We eventually ran out of money, so I had to borrow from family to keep my children in private school. I was mortified, exhausted, feeling like I was tearing at the seams, and I was still failing. The last straw was when the office manager told me I had to stop using Ubers to get to and from the airport. I said I couldn't, as a matter of safety. I was so out of it when I landed that driving would have been dangerous for me and for other people on the road. Her response? I had to make "other arrangements." I found another arrangement: I quit and started my own firm.

In 2015, I launched Carminati Law PLLC. I had a daughter about a year later in 2016. That interlude, although not financially profitable, gave me sanity. I slowly found balance and re-emerged a different person. Although I was now solely responsible for rainmaking, billing, balancing the firm's books, handling trust accounts and overseeing deadlines, I entered one of the least stressful periods of my life. Even when I had my daughter, as a solo practitioner, my life stayed peaceful. I was taking care of four children now, rotating through nannies who quit with a minute's notice. I would have become hysterical a few years ago if faced with the same situation, but now I took things in stride. What I had, which I had not had before, was control over my life. A weight that I had never noticed was there lifted from my shoulders.

Eventually, a lawyer in Aspen, Colorado asked me to become his partner, so I moved to the Roaring Fork Valley. Was the partnership a good one? No. I was underpaid, among other issues, and underappreciated. However, I refused to be overworked. I refused to take on everyone else's responsibilities. I created a boundary and held to it. And lo and behold, other lawyers we worked with appreciated me, complimented me, and relied on me. I didn't have to crush myself to get those accolades. The partnership eventually came to an acrimonious end. One of the reasons was that, again, he expected me to man the office all day while he went where he wanted, pretexting that he was "rainmaking." For the first time, I said "no" and walked away. I was done giving this profession, and other lawyers more than they deserved from me.

I now run The Woman's Lawyer, my re-invented law firm, work full-time at a commercial litigation firm, and am running for the Colorado State Senate. I've made numerous changes to my life and looking back, I should have made them a long time ago. Most importantly, I could have made these changes while working for others. The secret was to set my boundaries early on and to learn how to say "no." If I am not available, I am not available. If I have a school event for my children, it takes its place on my calendar like any other appointment would. I stopped using an alarm clock in the morning (I wake up at 6:15 a.m. anyway). I turned off email notifications on my computer and my phone. I meet with clients two mornings per week and I work on their matters the rest of the time. I don't answer phone calls after 6:00 p.m. and I don't check my work email over the weekend.

Have I achieved anything since implementing these measures? You be the judge. I finished my space law doctoral thesis, which is about to get published by a European publishing house; I became vice president of a local bar organization; I was appointed to a statewide community college board of directors by the governor; I started a blog; I worked on a bill; I am running for office; I am learning a new language; and I am building a law firm. I also come home to my children, spend weekends with them, drink tea staring at the Colorado mountains, and enjoy lunches on a park bench on beautiful days. I didn't have to enable other people crushing me in order to make it.

Other lawyers will take as much as they can from you if you let them. Don't let them; it's not worth it.

Maria-Vittoria "Giugi" Carminati is a women's advocate, an intersectional activist, and a blogger. She lives in Aurora, Colorado with her four children. Her husband splits his time between Houston, Texas, where they own a home, and Denver. She graduated law school in 2008 and is now at the helm of her own law firm, The Woman's Lawyer, based in Denver. She focuses on representing women, people of color, and members of the LGBTQ community. Her firm operates as a social justice firm, representing victims of domestic violence and sexual assault. To fund her work, she provides high-end legal services to other law firms. She speaks French, English, Italian, and Spanish. She is on the Colorado Community College Systems Board of Directors and serves as vice president of Denver MAMAs, an organization for lawyer moms. After spending five years at a Biglaw firm and two years at a boutique, she launched her firm for the first time in 2015. She formed a partnership in Aspen, Colorado from 2016 to 2017. She then moved to Denver and re-launched her firm as The Woman's Lawyer. Giugi's blog, *Argue Like a Girl*, addresses current events and popular culture from a feminist perspective, providing biting commentary and thoughtful analysis. She has an LLM in Space, Cyber & Telecommunications Law and a JSD in Space Law. Learn more about Giugi at www.thewomanslawyer.com and www.arguelikeagirl.com.

Lesson 11

● ● ● ●

EFFECTIVE ORGANIZATIONAL HABITS OPEN DOORS, INCLUDING THOSE THAT ALLOW YOU TO BE YOUR OWN BOSS

KELLY CARMODY

A good system shortens the road to the goal.

– ORISON SWETT MARDEN

As a teenager, I was an organizational mess. My room was such a disaster that when my father came into my room to investigate after hearing someone (my boyfriend) knocking on my window one night, he crawled through my room to make sure he did not trip over the piles of clothes, books, and other items on my floor. Although being scared to death by my dad – I had not heard him come in – should have encouraged me to change my ways, it did not. When I married my boyfriend four years later, it was he who prompted the beginning of my organizational transformation. He lived by the motto, *a place for everything and everything in its place.* I started hanging up my clothes in the closet, putting things away in their place, and began to appreciate some of the benefits of being organized.

Still, it was not until I started my career that the benefits of having good organizational skills were proven to me. Two of my first bosses were very successful leaders in civil legal aid. Both, however, had their desks, file cabinets, and floors covered by multiple, random stacks of memos, reports, notebooks, newspapers, and anything else that would "stack." They would spend valuable minutes, and sometimes hours, searching for needed information. I witnessed their lost productivity. If I was meeting with them about a project, I would wait for them to find information needed for our discussion, while watching and feeling *my* productivity slip away.

From these experiences, I learned to be the "organized one." I learned to file away information that could potentially be needed in the future. I became the go-to person for these bosses when they were looking for information. They learned to trust that if I had seen the information previously, I would have it or know where it was. Although this may have fed into their unorganized work style, I knew it was not in the cards for me to change their work habits.

One downside of my increasingly effective organizational skills may have been the tendency of a group to look to me to do the secretarial or administrative work, since I was the "organized one." It is difficult to determine whether this was because of my skills or because the members of work groups early in my career were predominately men and they were used to a woman taking on the secretarial duties. Although I do not believe it negatively affected my career, it is a side effect I have had to balance over time.

Fast-forward more than 30 years and I have learned that as important as my organizational skills were while an employee of civil legal aid organizations, they have been critical to my later career success as a national civil legal aid consultant. Being self-employed with no employees means I must deal with a wide variety of items on my to-do list every day. Working on multiple clients' projects in sometimes three different time zones while at the same time handling the administration of my office – billing, record-keeping, technology – takes all of my organizational skills to keep my business running smoothly—at least most of the time.

Benjamin Franklin said, "For every minute spent in organizing, an hour is earned." He was referring to an hour of time, which I have found to be true. As important, however, is that an hour can be earned to spend on activities that earn a fee. If I am organizing work that is *not* billable, that is freeing up time for work that *is* billable. If I am organizing work that *is* billable, that is saving the client money when my billable work for them is done more efficiently.

"Being organized," for me, includes at least these practices: using a daily to-do list; creating work plans for each project; keeping my emails organized in folders and subfolders; keeping my bookmarks organized in folders and subfolders; keeping paper files of documents that are much easier to read on paper; and making notebooks with tabs and tables of contents for compilations of documents that I refer to over time.

The thought processes that these and other organizing procedures take have led to my ability to do process or system analysis with clients to improve their efficiency. It is immensely satisfying to share my skills and knowledge with others and see their "aha" moment when they realize how much time they can save for themselves, their organizations and/or their clients. As critical as these efficiencies are to my bottom line as a solo consultant, they are equally critical to the nonprofit organizations that I work with that continually seek ways to squeeze more time for assistance to more clients.

I also have found good organizational skills are essential to managing projects. Being able to keep multiple components of a project moving forward at the right times takes organized information and systems. Having these skills is important to any lawyer, whether a consultant leading a client through a project or a litigator preparing a case for court.

Organizational skills encompass more than what I have described in this Lesson, but I have found the skills described here to be the foundation of much of my success as an employee and a consultant, and in life. Being organized has given me the time to learn, to plan, to communicate, to execute, and the time to enjoy life.

Kelly Carmody is the founder of Carmody and Associates which provides consulting services to civil legal aid providers, funders, and supporters. Her mission is to improve and expand the civil legal aid delivery system. Her primary areas of expertise include strategic planning, program evaluation, staff/pro bono delivery system development, process/organizational analysis and development, attorney recruitment and retention, compensation analysis and strategy, and management/board assistance.

Before opening Carmody and Associates, Kelly was a lobbyist for civil legal aid clients and a facilitator of civil legal aid's management and advocacy through statewide organizations in Kentucky, Tennessee, and Arizona, and nationally through the National Legal Aid & Defender Association, the National Health Law Program, and the Center on Budget and Policy Priorities.

Kelly received her B.S. degree from South Dakota State University, an M.S.W. from the University of Kentucky, and a J.D. from Georgetown University Law Center. She is licensed to practice law in Arizona and resides in Phoenix. Learn more about Kelly at www.carmodyandassociates.com.

Lesson 12

● ● ● ●

THREE THINGS I WISH I'D REMEMBERED AT THE START OF MY PRACTICE

KATHERINE E. CHARONKO

Nothing can bring you peace but yourself.

— *Ralph Waldo Emerson*

Practicing mindfulness and meditation were part of my childhood. I grew up in a family of communicators, counselors, and wonderful people who support their communities. I always wanted to help people; the question was how. Before I practiced law, I worked in professional theater. While maybe not a traditional pre-law profession, theater ignited my desire to pursue the law.

When I started law school, I knew I wanted to be there—I was there to help people. And I knew it would be hard. What I didn't know was that I would question being there. I didn't know how I would be helping people. And I didn't know how hard it would be.

When I am asked how I found my path or how I ended up interested in my current area of practice, electronic discovery, I respond that I found an area that engaged me and ran with it. When I am asked how I balance work and life, I explain that it isn't easy. I don't always find balance, which is OK.

PASSION: HOW IT CAN HELP YOU FIND YOUR PATH.

I remember when someone asked me, "Did you ever think you would be here?" My answer was, "It depends." Did they mean: (1) here as a lawyer, (2) here at my firm, or (3) here in a management role? The answer to all those questions is "yes." They weren't the first and they won't be the last person to ask if I am surprised that I am where I am. I'm not surprised to be where I am because I learned a secret early on, one that sometimes I forget along the way. I am the only one who can maintain my path. I was diagnosed in first grade with dyslexia. I never let that stop me from meeting my goals and making my own path in life. Passion has always guided me to my chosen path.

Simplistic in theory, monumental in practice. Other legal professionals have told me they don't know if they want to do "this" anymore. Hell, I've been there, too. What is often forgotten about passion is that it doesn't always burn bright every day. There will be days that you hate what you do. Passion keeps you going on those days. The path to legal passion was clear as mud for me. I graduated law school not knowing what I "wanted to do." My work with indigent clients steered me toward plaintiffs' litigation. Life, however, is not binary. I started at a boutique law firm (where I work to this day) that afforded me the opportunity to experience all aspects of practice.

When I found my passion, I also found my path. I took what kept me motivated and interested in electronic discovery and used it to develop my career. I took a passion and ran with it. You can, too.

PATIENCE: PRACTICE IT EVERY DAY.

You are not going to like everyone. Everyone is not going to like you. It is as simple as that. The lesson to learn is how not to outwardly show that dislike, and to practice stepping back and being mindful of others. In my pre-law life, I didn't contemplate the rigors involved in working at an office. Anyone who works in an office can understand these. I found myself forgetting early lessons about dealing with myself and others. Stress played a starring role in my early career. I found myself behaving in ways that were not normal for me. I forgot to practice patience. I sniped at others over trivial matters. I forgot to practice mindful breathing and meditation because I was "too busy."

It is never intentional to forget the lessons we learn about human interactions, but as humans, stress often guides our behavior. This was the case for me until one work trip when I found myself telling another attorney who was feeling excess stress about how growing up I was taught about mindfulness and the importance of practicing meditation. We talked mindful breathing and focusing your thoughts back to a quiet place. I was reminded of something I heard when I was in grade school: "[w]hatever the tasks, do them slowly and with ease, in mindfulness." It wasn't until much later in life that I came across that quote in a book by Thich Nhat Hanh called *The Miracle of Mindfulness: An Introduction to the Practice of Mediation.* This simple idea is one that I had to rediscover. The lessons that were a fundamental part of who I was were so easy to share with someone else. I had just forgotten them for myself. Stress doesn't go away, but taking stress out on yourself and others isn't the answer, either.

After that trip, I started to focus back on being an active listener and meditation. I opened myself back up to the understanding that everyone has more happening in their life than what I was seeing. This rediscovered philosophy refocused my agitated energy back to mindful energy. My stress dropped, and I was more focused. Now, I take proactive steps to manage my stress. I encourage you to do the same.

PEOPLE: FIND THEM. CONNECT WITH THEM. SPEND TIME WITH THEM.

Finding people is different for everyone. I found "my people" by reconnecting with lifelong friends, one of whom is now my husband. I found my people by spending time outside of work with colleagues who have become my friends. I found my people by staying in touch with my family. Humans need other humans. Our profession has a lot of causalities, especially when it comes to relationships. The only way to find people is to put yourself out there. Take a chance on yourself. Burnout is real, so make sure to take time for an adventure. I had forgotten this.

You need people in your life. You need your family. You need friends. You need colleagues. And you need to spend time with them outside of work. As attorneys, we often find ourselves "at work" more than we are at home. I found myself living my work most of my waking hours. Sometimes, I still live my work at odd hours of the night when I wake up worrying about this or that. But, the difference is now I practice turning work off when I'm at home (or at least reducing the impact work has on my home time). It is true—you need to find a balance between work and life.

When I started practicing full time, like so many other first-year associates, I felt I had to eat, breathe, and live my work 24/7. To some extent, this is true. But like so many others, I let my work affect my relationships outside of work. For me, the change came when my now-husband and I started taking extended vacations each summer. At first, I felt guilty being away from the office. On one of these trips I read a study about lawyer burnout, and it clicked for me. I couldn't stay on 24/7. I needed people in my life. I needed adventures. I needed to be out of the office.

I leave you with one final piece of advice: What works for me may not work for you. And that is OK. In the words of Abraham Lincoln, "I do the very best I know how – the very best I can; and I mean to keep doing so until the end." So should you. That is how you find your path. That is how you find your passion, your peace and, more often than not, your people.

Kate Charonko is a partner at Bailey & Glasser LLP where she focuses her practice mainly on complex litigation, e-Discovery and national plaintiff class actions. She serves as part of Bailey & Glasser's multidistrict litigation automotive and medical device product liability action teams as well as other multidistrict litigation matters across the country. In addition to her litigation work, Kate is the director of the firm's developing e-Discovery practice advising clients and attorneys regarding numerous aspects of e-Discovery. Kate graduated from West Virginia University College of Law. Upon graduation, she received the Order of the Barristers national honorary distinction for her written and oral advocacy skills. She is an active member of various legal and e-Discovery organizations. Learn more about Kate at www.baileyglasser.com.

Lesson 13

● ● ● ●

DON'T DO IT ALONE
MANDI CLAY

Walking with a friend in the dark is better than walking alone in the light.

— HELEN KELLER

Survey after survey shows that lawyers are disproportionately susceptible to mental health and addiction issues. These problems get worse with isolation. Being the only, or one of a few, female attorneys can add to this isolation. So, don't isolate yourself. Get out there and be someone that people expect to see, so that if you start isolating yourself someone might reach out to check on you. Be a name and face that people recognize; it makes you more accountable to yourself as well. You're less likely to isolate yourself if you feel that your absence from events will be noticed.

The best way to avoid isolation? Voluntary bar work. There's a belief that it is difficult to make friends after college, and that is probably true for a lot of people. But, of all the things that are difficult about being a lawyer, the opportunities it gives you to meet people and make friends are unparalleled in any other profession. My voluntary bar work has given me the strongest network, of mostly women, I could ever imagine. These are the people who found me a new job when the one I was in was unbearable; sent food and flowers to my home when my husband's brother died; came to and publicized my party kicking off my mediation practice; nominated me for awards; and just generally held me up professionally and personally.

Note, though, that I said voluntary bar *work*. Don't just be a joiner, paying dues and listing things on your bio without actually doing anything. Take a role, even a small one, and show people the kind of person you are—your commitment, your creativity, your empathy, your kindness. These are things that don't always shine through your legal work, especially to people who don't work directly with you. They are, however, the most important things. Getting involved in even the smallest of voluntary bars, or joining a state bar committee, will help you make friends and build a network. These friendships will keep you from being isolated and will become resources for your professional advancement. The business development benefits are side effects of the friendships you create. Both are invaluable.

I suffered from depression and panic disorder long before I became a lawyer, which gave me the benefit of learning how to cope before adding the stresses of the law to my life. One of those lessons is that people are more important than anything in this world. Medication and therapy are crucial elements of my mental health treatment, but my friends are just as crucial. You need people who notice when you're not yourself, people you can fall apart in front of, people who will stand as allies with you in uncomfortable situations, and people who can keep an eye on you when you can't be trusted to be alone.

As soon as I started in private practice, I began attending voluntary bar events, mostly because I felt compelled to make myself known to other lawyers. I started small, just attending a few events and meeting a few people. After a year or so I decided to do more. I emailed the incoming president of the local women lawyers association and asked to be on a committee. Well, guess what? She needed a public relations committee chair. Six years later and I am the vice president of that organization, looking toward being president elect and president in the next two years. I stand in the shoes of amazing women who have become judges, managing partners, and successful entrepreneurs. I stand in the path of greatness, thanks to a single email I sent when I was a baby lawyer.

I also never gave in to the law firm culture of working 24/7/365. Once you do, it is extremely difficult to walk it back—so set these boundaries early. I leave the office for lunch almost every day and come home in time for dinner with my family. I use my lunch breaks to go to voluntary bar events, to meet up with friends, and to talk to my family on the phone. Every lunch break is a connection to someone who thinks I'm awesome. How great does that sound? Spend an hour a day with someone awesome who thinks you are awesome, too. I use my Monday lunch dates to overcome my Sunday night dread. No matter how stressful the job is, how nasty my superiors or opposing counsel are to me, or how difficult a client is, I have a break and an escape. Most of my lunch dates are friends I made through my voluntary bar work.

Once you build these relationships, you will have a network of friends and connections who can be invaluable. I highly recommend asking your network for help when you need it, and recognition when you deserve it. Every year there are hundreds of awards given to lawyers across the country— and in almost all cases those awards start with a nomination. *Ask* your friends for those nominations. It is not egotistical, it is – in fact – less egotistical than just sitting back and expecting people to think of you for whatever award they hear about and then making the effort to nominate you. And no, you're not using them—as long as the friendship and your behavior are genuine. Lawyers are busy; we don't know all the awards available, all the deadlines or all the nomination processes. So, if I see an award that I think I'm qualified for, I ask someone to nominate me for it—and I ask them if there is something I can nominate them for. It starts with simple things—reaching out to the people you will be nominating for recognition and asking them to nominate you. I don't present it as a quid pro quo, just as a nudge to keep me in mind when filling out the form and letting them know which category I want to be considered in.

Getting involved with the legal community will bolster your self-confidence and increase your ability to market yourself. The best things that have happened in my life and career come from being bold and blatant. Introducing myself, asking for what I need or want, and letting people help me when they can. It definitely has to be a two-way street; you have to help others if you want them to help you, and you have to show that you are deserving of the things you want. But working yourself to death in your office with your head down is certainly not the road to happiness, and rarely the road to success. Look up, get out, stand out, and take advantage of the biggest asset the legal community has—the community itself.

Mandi Clay was born and raised in Buffalo, New York. She has been practicing law in Tampa for more than 10 years. She is the founder and managing attorney of Three Thirteen Law, PLLC. Mandi is a civil litigator with a bachelor's degree in criminal justice from Florida Atlantic University and her law degree from the University of Georgia School of Law. She is also a certified circuit court mediator and has experience in a variety of practice areas.

Mandi has experienced the practice of law from both sides of the bench, having clerked for U.S. District Judge Gregory A. Presnell and U.S. District

Judge Charlene Edwards Honeywell, both in the Middle District of Florida. She prides herself on being efficient and responsive to her clients and is dedicated to providing practical advice tailored to fit each client's specific goals.

Within the legal community, Mandi is well respected among both practitioners and the judiciary. She is an active member of several voluntary bar groups, is vice president of the Hillsborough Association for Women Lawyers, and serves on two Florida Bar committees: the Voluntary Bar Liaison Committee and the Standing Committee on Mental Health and Wellness of Florida Lawyers.

Mandi lives in Riverview, Florida with her husband, Korey, and is a very busy auntie to about 25 of her friends' children. Learn more about Mandi at www.threethirteenlaw.com.

Lesson 14

● ● ● ●

HONORING YOURSELF
SUSAN DAICOFF

Better one's own path, though uncertain, than the path of another well-made.

— UNKNOWN

ALWAYS DRESS FOR THE JOB YOU WANT NEXT, NOT THE JOB YOU HAVE NOW.

This may not be trendy or popular in today's business casual world, but it has stood me in good stead. It makes me feel more confident and capable. Someone may notice you and think, "She would be a good candidate for promotion to president/dean/director, etc." Do you want to move up with more responsibility? Do you think that your ideas might move your organization or firm forward into a brighter future? Treat yourself to an amazing wardrobe.

SPEND ENERGY WISELY ("BE THE WATER THAT FLOWS AROUND THE ROCK AND EVENTUALLY WEARS IT AWAY").

Women lawyers – still – apparently receive inappropriate and offensive words, looks, gestures, and actions, probably daily. It has taken me 38 years to acknowledge many situations in law school and practice that were wrong. I should have complained and may have had good causes of action. There's a balance here between honoring yourself and honoring how you spend your time and energy. There's no need to pretend that offensive things didn't occur or aren't occurring, but there's no need to wear oneself out, either. I choose to spend energy on my own personal goals and actions, which leads to the next point.

HOW YOU SPEND YOUR TIME AND ENERGY MATTERS. THEY ARE NOT UNLIMITED.

I came of age in the in the 1970s, the era of "Women's Lib." My first jobs were in the "male-dominated" workplaces of the 1980s. As my parents' oldest child, I was brought up as if I were male. The messages I received at home, school, and work were, tacitly and explicitly, "You don't need to focus on getting married and having children. You're not the domestic type. Get as many educational degrees as possible and look toward a professional career, the harder the better. Reach for the stars!" In the 1980s, women were told they could "have it all": a career, a home, children, a loving marriage, health, fame, fortune, status, and meaningful relationships. We wore ourselves out trying to get "it all." Now I realize, I can't "do it all" and "have it all" without some toll taken on my health, energy, relationships, sanity, or career progression. I've tried, multiple times, and failed. Twenty-two years ago, my children's father and I realized that we wanted him to stay home and raise the children while I "reached for the stars." I needed his tangible and intangible support and the kids needed his full-time parenting and his presence. I simply wasn't home—I was working, lecturing, traveling, writing…doing. The more he stayed home, the more successful I became professionally. This evolved, as there was no script or model for this at-the-time unusual lifestyle.

I no longer expect myself to "do it all": work full time as a lawyer, be a loving spouse, mother, daughter, sister, and friend, grocery shop, cook, clean, pay bills, manage finances, invest savings, plan for the future, manage repairs, cars, and lawn care, decorate, send gifts, clothes shop, exercise, meditate, pray, attend church, have a fun hobby, meet with friends for fun and support, plan vacations, read books, stay current with news and sports…whew! Maybe pick three. Collaborative law founder and lawyer Stu Webb gave me a set of "purpose cards" 20 years ago. I sort through them and select the three things in which I'm most interested at the moment. Some examples include: exercise, rest, and learning something new. Let go of unreasonable expectations and that mile-long "to-do" list. Focus on three reasonable things, plus something fun. Or, simply let go and ask a higher source to guide and direct your actions for the day. I try to do things that I value, not rush around in a panic. A favorite friend says, "What you do matters, how you spend your time matters, your time and energy are not unlimited." This has become a mantra.

JOB OR NO JOB, I AM STILL ME.

Who would you be if you had never become a lawyer? That question, asked years ago by clinical psychologist and mentor Dr. Clint Bowers, left me dumbfounded with no answer. I had no "me" without my law license. Today, I have lost and found amazing jobs in the legal profession, tried out other professions, and am reasonably satisfied with whatever I'm doing. I feel as though I have a "me" today outside of being a lawyer.

When I was in high school, my senior "quote" in the yearbook was, "I want to help people." As a corporate, securities, and tax lawyer, I most valued helping new entrepreneurs start and grow businesses. I know I must incorporate some aspect of helping people into my workday or I am not going to stay in the job. Law professor Lawrence Krieger, a well-known expert on lawyer well-being and satisfaction, has empirically demonstrated that lawyer well-being is related to a connection between one's work and one's intrinsic values. Intrinsic values are what drives you—those things you enjoy so much that they keep you coming back. They may be different for everyone. Some examples are: creativity, innovation, having independence, autonomy, defending people's rights, doing justice, righting wrongs, being an example to your family and community, and running your own business. Identify yours—and then be sure you have some element of that activity in your work—weekly, if not daily.

When my intrinsic values were writing, public speaking, and changing the legal profession, I wrote regularly, planning a major work and many talks annually. Later, I began to want to practice law as a healing profession. Five years ago, I began spending four hours a week at the homeless shelter— half legal work and half playing music. Doing this work made everything else different, better. I began taking on legal work that had a rehabilitative, healing, positive effect on clients' lives, until most of my legal work had some intrinsic value to me (e.g., helping entrepreneurs, helping veterans, helping end homelessness, solving problems, training law students to practice law as a healing profession).

DEVELOPMENTAL PSYCHOLOGIST ERIK ERICKSON HAD IT RIGHT.

In graduate psychology school, I learned that there are distinct stages in life during which different things are important. In my 20s, I worked hard in male-dominated, challenging areas of the law to prove I could be just as tough and smart as anyone. This age is focused on becoming self-sufficient and, then, on intimate relationships. In my 30s and 40s, I wanted to set and reach a personal goal, career-wise, which connects perfectly to the Ericksonian stage of Career Consolidation (focused on "developing a 'career' characterized by commitment, compensation, contentment, and competence"). I diligently climbed the ladders and reached the personal bests and goals I set for myself, until I found myself sitting, figuratively, on the top of the mountain, wondering, "what's next?" In my 50s, I sense a different set of goals and values developing. Developmental psychology calls this next stage, Generativity versus Stagnation, where the focus is on "...concern for establishing and guiding the next generation." I feel motivated to create legacies for the next generation of lawyers and clients. When values and drives change, it is all perfectly normal. Accepting the developmental stages gracefully and embracing the tasks and lessons of each stage have helped me relax, understand myself, and appreciate my career trajectory.

Susan Daicoff is a lawyer, mediator, author, and speaker. She was a law professor for 23 years including four years as a clinical director. She taught contracts, mediation clinic, general practice rehabilitative clinics, entrepreneurship clinic, professional responsibility, law as a healing profession, taxation, and law and psychology. With a J.D. (Honors, University of Florida), LL.M. Taxation (New York University), and M.S. Clinical Psychology (University of Central Florida), she also practiced transactional law and psychotherapy, prior to becoming a professor. Her main areas of expertise address lawyer personality, lawyer well-being, and law as a healing profession (therapeutic jurisprudence, restorative justice, collaborative law, preventive law, and the "comprehensive law movement"). Learn more about Susan at www.susandaicoff.webs.com.

Lesson 15

● ● ● ●

DO WHAT YOU LOVE

DANIELLE DavisRoe

Stepping onto a brand-new path is difficult, but not more difficult than remaining in a situation, which is not nurturing to the whole woman.

— MAYA ANGELOU

If you don't love your job, it is time to consider a career change. You might not have to look as far as you might think to find a rewarding alternative career. Many attorneys no longer excited by the prospect of walking into the office or courtroom every day have found satisfaction just outside of the practice of law. Your license is still valuable, even if you leave the actual practice of law.

I was working in a small specialty law firm when I started dreading going to work every day. The dread crept in; it didn't happen overnight. In fact, it took me months to realize that the career I worked so hard for just wasn't a good fit for me. After months of convincing myself to get out of bed and drive to work, I realized I needed to make a change. After spending three years in law school, I was hesitant to even consider leaving my career as an attorney.

Even though I grew weary of practicing law, there was one part of my job that I absolutely loved; I loved updating the firm's templates with new language and finding ways to improve the firm's efficiency. I often thought to myself long before I became disenchanted with the practice of law that I wished I could work on our templates and processes full time without meeting with clients, doing to court, and giving legal advice.

It never occurred to me, however, that such a job might exist and that I should look for it. I stumbled upon a job posting for a legal technology consultant specializing in document automation while I was perusing job postings on my law school's career services website after a particularly bad day at work. The job I had been dreaming of not only existed, but there was an opening that actually wanted someone with a license to practice law. If I had not been randomly looking through job postings on the day that I did, I never would have known that my dream career was a possibility.

Even though I was pretty sure that I had found my dream career, leaving the practice of law was scary. I knew I needed out, but I was afraid to admit that to other people. I was worried they would see me as a failure for spending so long chasing one dream, just to change directions a few years into my career. Most people don't understand what I do now as a legal technology consultant, but most have been very supportive.

I now consider myself a "recovering attorney." I maintain my license, but I don't practice law (other than the occasional demand letter for a friend). My company works exclusively for law firms and legal departments, so my license is valued by both my employer and my clients. Attorneys like working with other attorneys, even if the matter they are tackling is not a legal matter. My clients value that I have been there before. I know the challenges that law firms face. The importance of client confidentiality and court deadlines is not lost on me.

Most people go to law school to become "trusted advisors." Those may not be words commonly spoken by law students and practicing attorneys, but that really is the underlying goal of most attorneys. Attorneys want their clients to trust them and lean on them for advice no matter what life throws at them. Even if the attorney just refers the client to another attorney who specializes in the client's issue at hand, the attorney still wants to be trusted to make that referral.

As a legal technology consultant, I may not be giving out legal advice, but my relationship with my clients is the same. I am their trusted advisor. I don't just automate their estate planning documents, I advise them on the process they use for drafting documents and the software they use to do it. Sometimes my clients come to me with questions that I can't answer. Just like an attorney, when I can't give the advice they need, I refer them to another consultant who is an expert in the area where they need help. The relationship is the same in the end, I'm just not giving my clients legal advice.

Changing careers midstream was the best decision I could have made. I could have spent my life as a lawyer, convincing myself to get out of bed and go to work every day and I would have been reasonably successful. However, with a career that inspires me and allows me to grow and change, I have found that I am already more successful than I probably ever would have been as an attorney.

Success comes naturally when you love what you do. It is easy to go the extra mile or volunteer to learn something new on your own time when the work is enjoyable. I work more hours as a consultant than I ever did as attorney, but it doesn't feel like I'm working any harder. The work I do is appreciated more, and I am having more of a positive impact on the world than I could have had as a single attorney. Attorneys make their clients' lives better. I make attorneys' lives better, allowing them to help more people, which multiplies the effect I have on the world.

If I hadn't admitted to myself that my career as an attorney was not the right fit for me, I still would be trapped in a job that I didn't find fulfilling. If I hadn't stumbled across a job posting that I wasn't looking for, I never would have found my dream job. Don't be afraid to broaden your job search to jobs that don't traditionally require a license to practice law. Searching for jobs in your city generally may help you realize that your dream job is one you didn't even know existed before finding the job posting.

While most people find their next job by networking, if you aren't happy in your career and aren't sure what you want to do, it is worth the time to search online and submit applications to people you don't know. You might just get lucky and find the perfect opportunity for you.

Danielle DavisRoe is a senior consultant for Affinity Consulting Group, where she specializes in document automation, training, and process analysis. Danielle works out of Affinity's Columbus, Ohio, office, but travels around the country to provide software training and help firms analyze and improve their processes and technology. Prior to coming to Affinity, Danielle practiced as a family law attorney. Danielle graduated from The Ohio State University Fisher College of Business, *cum laude*, with a Bachelor of Science degree in business administration with a focus in economics and a minor in professional writing. She is also a graduate of The Ohio State University Moritz College of Law, *magna cum laude*, where she served as the Symposium Edition administrative editor on the *Entrepreneurial Business Law Journal* and as a public service fellow. Additionally, she received The Judge Joseph H. Harter Memorial Award for excellence in trial practice and is a member of the Order of the Coif. Learn more about Danielle at www.affinityconsulting.com.

Lesson 16

● ● ● ●

THERE'S ME AND THERE'S ME AND THERE'S ME: IT MAY BE TOO MUCH, BUT TOO LITTLE OF ME IS NOT ENOUGH

MICHELE DeSTEFANO

You're different and different – then you're different again.

– HENRY JAMES, FROM THE WINGS OF THE DOVE

They say good things come in threes. I hope "they" are right because there are three of me.

There's *Me*: the personal *Me*. The romantic who will drink a bottle of wine with you in the middle of the day and walk in the rain in Central Park holding your hand. The friend who will laugh at stupid jokes because it feels good to laugh. The *Me* who takes risks, jumps without thinking, takes a trip on a whim, who dreams big, and cries hard. There is silly *Me* who gets lost in a paper bag driving to the same place I've been before. And don't forget rash *Me* who says things I don't mean in the heat of the moment and who takes them back right away (*OK, eventually*), and then there's forever-faithful, loyal *Me* who will forgive fast and often—over and over again.

Then there's second *Me*, the maternal *Me*, the *Me* I grew into over time. The *Me* who thinks before I act and protects and defends you against attack, who holds your hair back from your face when you are sick. The *Me* who cuddles with you as we watch some show in which I have no interest. The *Me* who checks in on you without being asked, who *knows* without being told, who answers the phone in the middle of the night and *really* listens—even when you repeat what you say. The *Me* who knows you are lying and loves you just the same. This *Me* has your back. This *Me* is also the one who will believe you when no one else will. This *Me* is the one who puts up with everything and puts out what it takes to hold everything together—all while on a conference call with that other *Me*: the third *Me*.

Me-three is an altogether different *Me*, one who I created after graduating from college because I thought I was supposed to, because that's what everyone did, because it worked better that way. The third *Me*, the "work *Me*," was supposed to think, to act, and to most certainly appear differently. With nylons, heels, and hair pinned back, third-*Me* spoke in measured tones, waited my turn, respected hierarchies and walls, and prayed desperately no one would realize that the other two *Me*s were wild, crazy, clueless, and often lost (both figuratively and literally). The third *Me* loved praise (and money) and promotions (and money). The third *Me* wanted respect and recognition and to make it to the top—and would conform to do so. The third *Me* wanted to check boxes and see improvement that could be plotted on an X/Y graph. The third *Me* wanted to have it all. The third *Me* wanted to get the children ready for school, show up for work unruffled and on-time despite the sibling fighting, the spilled orange juice, and the sticky pancake syrup on the collar of my shirt (that I tried to lick off with my finger). The third *Me* wanted to be seen as a Wonder Woman—someone detail-oriented but someone who could see the forest through the trees; someone bright, organized, and with vision; someone with a computer by day and a family of five around a table eating a home-cooked meal at night as her loving spouse toasted her brilliance (and patted the perfect black lab nearby who was definitely NOT begging for table scraps). In reality however, my third *Me*? Well, she was an epic mess.

She was tired, short-tempered, and forever feeling inadequate. She was not just physically thin, she was thin-skinned as well. My third *Me* had a detectable shrill timbre in her voice that had not always been there. And the third *Me* hated the weakness in my other *Me*s, despite the fact that this 'weakness' was what also made the other *Me*s 'human' and relatable. My third *Me* yelled at the first two *Me*s as they cried at night behind closed doors because they were doing nothing very well. "*Stop your whining!*" third *Me* would scream to the other two. My third *Me* hated the stupid TV dramas that portrayed the happy working mom, successfully married with children and a full array of girlfriends from all eras of her life. To hold back the tears, third *Me* assuaged herself: "*Yeah right. No one has all that.*" My third *Me* (the resentful *Me*) scoffed at the stay-at-home-moms for their trips to Target and the brownies they brought to homeroom for Halloween. But gradually, I let third *Me* give way to the other *Me*s in *Me*.

Third *Me* still exists. But third *Me* does not exist on her own; instead, I bring all three *Me*s with me all the time: to work, at home, and everywhere else in my life. And this has made all the difference. I live in a world that does not seek work-life balance nor even what millennials seek: work-life integration. I live in a world where there are no walls between *Me*-one, *Me*-two, and *Me*-three. I live in a world without walls – literally and figuratively – and here's why: I started a program called LawWithoutWalls (LWOW) at the University of Miami School of Law. LWOW was designed to break down the walls between academics and students, between lawyers and business professionals, between schools of different rank and lawyers from different cultures.

I had a big dream and I needed every *Me* to make it come true. And the only way to have all of *Me* was to break down the walls between *Me* and my various self-concepts: my personal self, my maternal self, and my work self. (Paul J. Brouwer wrote eloquently about the dynamics of our self-concepts in his 1964 article *The Power to See Ourselves* for the HARVARD BUSINESS REVIEW.) And so, I set out to develop a place that was like what urban sociologist Ray Oldenberg calls a "third place": not the home, not the office, but something altogether different, where people from different disciplines and all walks of life come together. I developed LWOW as a third place—and most definitely not on my own. I co-developed it with people from all of my *Me*-spaces. I invited colleagues from work, I invited friends and family and my significant other (along with ex-lovers and even my ex-husband) to be a part of building and growing LWOW and, in so doing, my friends became work colleagues in LWOW, and my work colleagues in LWOW became my friends.

By taking part in LWOW, my friends and family gained an understanding of and appreciation for my work. Now, even my children have spent late nights scrambling to prepare presentations or to prep an event space with me. And that has brought my friends, my family, my colleagues, and my three *Me*s even closer together. Over time (and yes, it took time), as I asked those who joined me to break down the walls between them—between lawyer and client, between mentor and mentee, between partner and associate, and between lawyers from competing firms—I learned to do the same with my *Me*s. Eventually, (and yes, it was eventually) I brought all of myself—personal, maternal, and work—together into one space and broke down the walls between them. So now there's *Me*, and *Me*, and *Me*, and we are one in the same. While I still make mistakes all the time, I no longer beat myself up about it, and neither do my work colleagues, or my family, or my friends, because they are one in the same—and we are all in this together.

They say good things come in threes. The three *Mes*? They agree. And they are OK with being "different and different—then…different again."

Michele DeStefano is a professor at the University of Miami School of Law, guest faculty at Harvard Law School, and the founder of LawWithoutWalls, a multidisciplinary, international think-tank of more than 2,000 lawyers, business professionals, entrepreneurs, and law and business students who create innovations at the intersection of law, business, and technology. Michele has been recognized by the ABA as a Legal Rebel and is also co-curator of the *Compliance Elliance Journal*, an e-journal of articles in compliance and ethics. Michele is an author, speaker, consultant, and facilitator on innovation, culture creation, teaming, and cross-practice, cross-border initiatives. Through her company MoveLaw, Michele runs bespoke, experiential learning workshops grounded in a human-centered design to transform how lawyers collaborate and create culture change.

Michele researches and writes about the growing intersections between law, business, and legal innovation. Her book, *Legal Upheaval: A Guide to Creativity, Collaboration, and Innovation in Law*, leverages more than 100 interviews with general counsels at international corporations and heads of innovation at law firms. Michele earned her B.A. (sociology and English), *magna cum laude*, from Dartmouth and her J.D., *magna cum laude*, from Harvard Law School. Learn more about Michele at www.LawWithoutWalls.org.

Lesson 17

● ● ● ●

DECIDING

DARBY DICKERSON

Every problem is an opportunity in disguise.

– *JOHN ADAMS*

Because making decisions is a part of life and leadership, a decision-making doctrine is indispensable. Below are principles from my own doctrine, which has been developed over decades of making decisions, evaluating the results, and learning from others.

CHOOSE THE RIGHT LENS.

Choose the right lens or perspective. As a law school dean, my touchstone is to make decisions that advance my school's best interest. Stated differently, I shouldn't advance my own interests, or the interests of any person or group, over the school's overall interest.

TIMING MATTERS.

People sometimes invoke "emergency" to prod you to act quickly. Avoid "catastrophization" (the tendency to blow things out of proportion) and separate real deadlines from false ones. Few deadlines are immovable. Consequently, even if someone presents you with a "hard" deadline, if you've not been given a reasonable time to decide, explore an extension.

But when true emergencies occur, be prepared to respond. Ensure you have appropriate policies and procedures in place, review them regularly, and train rigorously by holding table tops, simulations, or drills. Determine what information – such as contact information and key documents – you will need when the emergency strikes and make that information available in advance to those who will need it.

DEVELOP A STRONG PROCESS.

Even when your choices range from "bad" to "worse," a strong decision-making process can help you reach the best result. Identify the specific problem or question that needs to be resolved. Failing to refine the issue can result in a decision that doesn't address the real problem.

Establish and rank criteria. Criteria might include legal and regulatory compliance, financial costs, return on investment, ability to implement, timing, employee morale, and reputational impact. Decide how you will use criteria to evaluate alternatives and define "success."

Gather relevant data and information. Research similar situations that might have occurred in the past. Also, consider situations that don't initially seem on point, but might impact how you evaluate the issue.

Decision-making usually isn't a solo act. Build diverse teams with people who have different perspectives. Don't rely on people who agree with any idea you present. Engage the introverts. Silence the leader so others can share more freely, and de-incentivize information silos and hoarding.

ANTICIPATE.

Before deciding, always anticipate the consequences. What are the possible outcomes, and why? If we are missing a piece of information, how might that gap impact the outcome? If we change a fact, how might that shift affect the decision?

To help visualize the anticipation concept, consider the movie *Searching for Bobby Fischer,* in which the chess grandmaster instructs his young prodigy, who is partial to speed chess, "Don't move until you figure it out in your head." When the student objects, saying he can't figure it out unless he actually moves the pieces, the grandmaster – in dramatic fashion – sweeps the board clear. Later, in a championship match, the student repeats to himself, "Don't move until you see it." The teacher's advice wasn't to be indecisive, but to anticipate the various moves, and implications of those moves, before actually moving.

An effective "anticipation" exercise is what I've dubbed "The Rule of 10." Just days after I became associate dean at Stetson Law, a student rushed into my office. She had a job interview the next day and needed a transcript. But her account was on hold. Attempting to help, I lifted the hold for one day so the student could get her transcript for the interview. Word quickly spread about this policy deviation, and I ended up with a line of students outside my door seeking a similar accommodation. The better answer to the student would have been, "Let me check on the situation and review our policy, and I'll be back in touch with you as quickly as possible. What's the best way to reach you between now and 4:00 p.m.?" That response would have given me time to consider the Rule of 10.

The Rule is simple: If you are going to grant someone's request, you must be prepared to do the same for the next 10 people who seek the same thing. If you're not, don't grant the request but instead consider other alternatives.

RESIST "DELEGATING UP."

Leaders are often skilled problem solvers. But leaders must be careful not to make decisions that others should be making. When someone below – or next to – you on the organizational chart asks you to decide, first consider whether you or the other person is the correct decision-maker. If the other person should make the decision, empower them to do so.

If you're not the leader, resist the temptation to delegate up. If you're not sure it's your decision to make, ask. And if you're not comfortable deciding outright, present your supervisor with a recommendation, or with options accompanied by pros and cons.

ACTUALLY DECIDE.

At the right point, decide. Along the way, I've worked with people who – for a variety of reasons including fear of criticism or deciding incorrectly, procrastination, perfectionism, or disorganization – routinely avoid deciding.

Use your process. Have confidence in your judgment. Understand that few decisions are perfect. But also understand that most decisions aren't irreversible and can be modified or retracted if the consequences weren't what you expected.

That being said, inaction can be a decision. Indeed, sometimes, you shouldn't act; it's not the right time, you're not the correct decision-maker, or you simply don't have the right information or tools to act. But learn to recognize when inaction is a deliberate decision as opposed to an avoidance technique.

COMMUNICATE.

Selecting when and how to communicate the decision can influence success. When sharing the decision, explain not just the who, what, when, and where, but also the how and why.

Explaining why you made a particular decision will help others understand, accept, and hopefully embrace it. Conversely, omitting your rationale can increase the chance that more people will question your motives. Also, making your "how" – the decision-making process – transparent will increase the odds of people accepting, or at least respecting, your decision.

When you cannot share the how or why – such as when the attorney-client privilege applies or because key information is private – explain why you can't share. Not only will most people appreciate that effort, but sharing why you can't share more can help build trust and confidence.

BE ACCOUNTABLE.

If a decision was not as good as you had hoped, acknowledge that. Then try again. We often make the greatest progress after a failure.

DON'T RESIST CHANGING COURSE.

Few business decisions are irreversible. If you decide and the consequences aren't acceptable, change course. When you need to change a decision, return to the lens principle: Don't focus on whether you might be embarrassed by having to retract or modify a decision. Instead, focus on the best interests of your organization or client. Then, evaluate both the result and the process before issuing the new decision.

SEEK OPPORTUNITY.

Progress is really a series of decisions. Decisions, made one by one, can transform organizations or projects. One of my favorite sayings is "Every problem is an opportunity in disguise." If you focus on the opportunity instead of the challenge, even difficult decisions can become gratifying to make.

Darby Dickerson is the dean and a professor of law at The John Marshall Law School in Chicago. She has previously served as the dean and W. Frank Newton Professor of Law at Texas Tech University School of Law and vice president and dean at Stetson University College of Law. She earned her B.A. and M.A. from The College of William & Mary and her J.D. from Vanderbilt Law School. She clerked on the U.S. Court of Appeals for the Sixth Circuit and practiced litigation with the firm now known as Locke Lord in Dallas, Texas. Learn more about Darby at www.jmls.edu.

Lesson 18

• • • •

OWN WHO YOU ARE

KATY GOSHTASBI

Hurt people hurt people. That's how pain patterns get passed on, generation after generation after generation. Break the chain today. Meet anger with sympathy, contempt with compassion, cruelty with kindness. Greet grimaces with smiles. Forgive and forget about finding fault. Love is the weapon of the future.

— YEHUDA BERG

Everyone has a great story that can inspire others and drive success. Everyone's story is just as important and impactful as the next person's story. Without our stories, our impact and success are minimized.

My story of success starts as a 6-year-old girl in Iran. When the revolution hit Iran in 1979, we knew we were not welcome there anymore as a religious minority. We decided to leave for a short bit until the unrest died down. We packed two suitcases and flew to Indiana, thinking we'd be gone for a few weeks. We never went back to Iran.

I was blessed to grow up in a wonderful suburb of Indianapolis with very kind and accepting people. But I was beaten up as a kid because I looked different than all the other Midwestern kids. Kids are not nice to other kids necessarily. It hurt and it angered me. I felt alone at times. It was tough to be different.

Fast-forward a few years. I always wanted to be a securities lawyer. Two reasons: 1) I wanted to save the world, and I thought being a lawyer was the way to do so; and 2) I wrongly thought that maybe, if I was a lawyer, people would love and accept me more.

So, I put myself through undergraduate college and law school. I had a wonderful career as a securities lawyer, mostly in Washington, D.C. First, I was a federal lobbyist on Capitol Hill. I lobbied for state securities laws. I saw first-hand the ugly truth of the old saying: "Laws are like sausages. It's better not to see them being made." At the time, I was wide-eyed and so idealistic. I still am idealistic, only now I know what it really means to use my idealism as a tool to serve humanity.

Following my work as a lobbyist, I got my dream job at the Securities & Exchange Commission (SEC). I was humbled to work with such great minds every day at the SEC. I was there during the Enron cleanup post-Sarbanes-Oxley and Bernie Madoff.

I remember the day I appeared before the SEC chairman and commissioners arguing for a rule I had helped draft. CNN and all the major networks were covering the hearing. Substantively, it went well. When we took a break, a respected colleague of mine in private practice who was in the audience came up to me to congratulate me. I still remember his words so clearly: "Never mind the substance, Katy. Your hair and suit look so great, even from back where I'm sitting." I was taken aback. My first instinct was to be offended. But he looked so sincere and genuinely proud of me. I stopped and took it as a compliment. Was there more to success than substantive knowledge?

My next position was with a major law firm with offices in Washington, D.C. I was surrounded by men almost twice my age, but I developed strong professional relationships with them. I would wine and dine and plan events. Other lawyers would ask me for advice on how I got promoted or how I got "that assignment." I took a lot of these lawyers to lunch and shared with them what I was doing. I was giving branding advice, but I just didn't know it.

Soon I had another choice to make. I could stay in D.C. and have a great time, or I could move to California to be closer to my family. I chose to move. I took my last legal job as in-house counsel at a large insurance company. I had come full circle and had been around the entire legal arena.

Then I burned out. It hit me the day I had spent 15 hours drafting a tiny part of a mutual fund prospectus. I went home at nine o'clock that night and opened my inbox to find my own prospectus. I reflexively threw the prospectus away because no one reads that stuff. I no longer felt I was of service to humanity. That's the moment I knew I had to move on from my legal career if I wanted to be happy, live longer, thrive, and contribute to society. It was a personal decision. I was scared and confused, yet oddly very clear.

So, I switched careers and found my natural talent and strength in what I do now. Every day I'm grateful to do what I do and to make a contribution.

As a growth, change, and branding expert, I believe in success every day. I believe success is easier than we think it is. Here are the main tips I give to all my clients, whether I'm conducting a law firm retreat, working with partners in a training, or in my current role as chair of the ABA Law Practice Division.

1. Own it. This is my favorite phrase and one I use often with clients. Before anyone believes us to be an expert in any field, we must first believe in ourselves. So, do you believe you are good at what you do as a woman lawyer? Do you believe you are an expert in your space? If so, then use your expertise and share it with everyone more often. Trust your gut. If it feels good, then you can own it. If it doesn't feel good, don't do it. Don't even bother. You won't "own" it well.

2. Show up and be ready to be seen as yourself. I've observed that as women, we often don't show up. When we do, we don't always show up as our best, genuine, and authentic self. It's easy to get sucked into the problem of competing with the opposite gender. When I practiced law in Washington, D.C., I saw many women lawyers (including myself at times) try to compete with men by trying to look and behave more like a man. We would wear dark pant suits and pretend that we were like men. It was painful and didn't get results. The men didn't respect us, and other women competed harder with us. All it did was drive up stress and reduce self-confidence.

Only genuine brands win. If you are going to show up, show up as your best self. If you want to wear a skirt, go for it. If you stand out and look good in pink or a floral print, please do so. Makeup is fine. At conferences, having makeup on allows the audience to see your features and facial gestures better from afar. So, it possibly enhances communication. There's nothing more powerful, attractive, and credible than a person who knows who they are and shows up as their best self.

3. Bring your unique natural strengths to the game. Each of us has one thing we do so easily that we don't necessarily realize others may not do it as well. We take our natural ability for granted. And oftentimes, it has nothing to do with our actual legal expertise. Identifying and deliberately using your natural strength makes you feel good about yourself because you are at ease. This then puts you in a place where you resonate even more powerfully with your audience and are seen as even more credible and influential.

You've got this! I promise.

Katy Goshtasbi is a growth, change, and branding expert and founder of Puris Consulting. She works with law firms, lawyers, and organizations on growing in size and profits by mastering change and developing brands that get their message out effectively. The results include happier, more productive lawyers, reduced stress, better clients, and increased revenues. Katy is a nationally recognized professional speaker and trainer, traveling the globe sharing her knowledge. She is the author of *Personal Branding 101: Develop Your Personal Brand with Ease* and *Personal Branding in One Hour For Lawyers.* She practiced securities law for over 14 years and served as chair of the ABA Law Practice Division in 2018-2019. Learn more about Katy at www.purisconsulting.com.

Lesson 19

● ● ● ●

CHOOSE YOUR OWN ADVENTURE: DECISIONS, PIVOTS, AND POSSIBILITIES

IVY B. GREY

Don't cling to a mistake just because you spent a lot of time making it.

—AUBREY DE GREY

In our legal careers, we buy into the notion that there is only one path. We imagine a well-marked, perfectly manicured, tranquil path that will lead us to success, if we only stay the course. Then we live in fear of being forced off that path due to some mistake. We imagine that anything outside of that path is a raging river of hot lava and certain doom. But what if straying from that path led you to something better?

Rather than embracing our childhood games of "hot lava" and vigorously avoiding stepping out of bounds, I think we should turn to another childhood game for direction: *Choose Your Own Adventure* gamebooks.

Choose Your Own Adventure was an interactive series of books published from 1979 to 1998. They were told in the second person, which made the reader the protagonist in charge of charting the course that the story would take. Every few pages the reader would need to make a decision to move forward.

They were popular because they gave young readers a sense of power and ownership over the narrative. But they also forced readers to make decisions based on the evidence available and make the best out of it. Yet, the outcomes were often random. Often, the safest decisions didn't lead to the best results. This was meant to give a realistic sense of unpredictability, which was fun and interesting. While the reader was stuck with their decision during that reading, readers were always encouraged to re-read the book, make different choices, and follow a different path to a different ending.

When reading a *Choose Your Own Adventure* book, you felt a sense that decisions had consequences, but there was also the freedom to choose again. While it was the end of *that* story and *that* path, it wasn't the end of the book.

THREE LESSONS FROM *CHOOSE YOUR OWN ADVENTURE* BOOKS

I learned three key lessons from *Choose Your Own Adventure* books that have freed me from fear and a limited path in law and helped me to redefine how I can contribute to this profession.

First, I am the protagonist. I am free to write my own character description and that character is not required to carry the baggage of earlier descriptions. I get to direct this life and these decisions.

Second, decisions that determine direction are a constant part of life. Life is not one decision that sets an unchangeable course. Instead, there are many decisions and many directions. Periodically, you must choose, and things could change. Embrace it.

Third, good decisions don't always lead to good results. Sometimes the safe decision driven by fear leads somewhere bad. And sometimes the risky decision driven by hope or curiosity leads somewhere great. But you don't know if you don't decide.

CHOOSING YOUR OWN PATH IN LAW

Legal careers have a variety of paths, endings, and stops along the way. Success need not be defined the same way for every person who obtains a law degree. Even when you share a goal with another person, your methods to achieve it can vary. You have the power to define your path and your goals— and you are responsible for your decisions along the way. Believe it or not, there is freedom and adventure in creating a life in the law.

Most of us imagine a linear path where we start our careers as associates and eventually become partners in a law firm. We expect that we will work long hours, do "good work," serve on a few firm and bar association committees, write a couple of articles, and then we'll get there. What if you could release yourself from the fear and expectation that you must follow this singular narrow path to succeed? What if you could do something different?

If you want to be lawyer, consultant, influencer, or innovator, you must build recognition. Contrary to what we've been led to believe, you can build your name outside of standard law firm channels. Write, blog, speak, or tweet. Pick any approach and use your voice. So long as you are knowledgeable or learning, your voice is worth hearing. Just be meaningful and authentic with your engagement. It takes a while to gain traction, but it does happen if you keep at it.

You can also be a creator. You can develop a process or create a product. There are many paths available. Examine your experience for how you can contribute and what unique skills or approaches you have. Freely offer your ideas. Consider joining forces with someone to expand or modify an existing process or product.

You can develop your reputation and determine your path outside the standard one. With technology, social media, affinity groups, and interest groups, you can develop influence and reach apart from limited law firm channels. By writing, blogging, speaking, engaging in social media, hosting or participating in podcasts, teaching, and sharing with others, you can carve out your place in the legal knowledge economy on your own terms.

Taking an uncharted course can be rewarding, but you must be persistent. At each juncture, you will be faced with decisions. Each decision will lead you on a new adventure—then you can decide again. Just like in the *Choose Your Own Adventure* books, some decisions will be as straightforward as stay or go. Own your decisions and embrace your adventure.

FINDING MY PATH IN LAW

My route to law and to legal technology was accidental and indirect. This was not the life I imagined for myself at 14, 18, 24 or even 30. But it has been a rewarding adventure. When you look at the elements of my life out of context, they seem random. But when you put them together, you see how I collected critical skills and experience to become a legal technology entrepreneur and help to reshape how lawyers deliver legal services. Each of those decisions and experiences made it possible to do what I am doing today.

I took a circuitous route to law that involved work in IT, journalism, and public relations. I went to law school because I wanted to find a new way to use my writing and research skills, my ability to anticipate opposition, and my thirst for fast pace and high stakes.

Prior to law school, and entirely by coincidence, I found bankruptcy law and I fell in love with it. Ultimately, I became a corporate bankruptcy lawyer in 2008—just in time for the recession. I have passionately lived this dream for 10 years in three different states.

During this time, I also received my LLM in corporate bankruptcy. And it was my LLM thesis that led me to legal technology. Upon hearing me fret about proofreading my thesis, a friend asked me to try his proofreading add-in for Microsoft Word. I did and could see its potential if it were modified to be a better fit for lawyers. That friend was PerfectIt founder Daniel Heuman, who asked me to join him and build the solution that I envisioned. The result is American Legal Style, a proofreading and editing app for lawyers that corrects hard-to-find mistakes ranging from typos and terms of art to *Bluebook* errors.

I've continued to practice law while creating American Legal Style and I've also written (and tweeted) my way to thought leadership in the legal technology community. This is not the life that I had planned, but I am happier than I could have imagined.

At each point during this journey, I had to decide to stay the course or try something new and exciting. Not everything worked out as planned, but I got to re-evaluate my character description, let go of baggage that was holding me back and make new decisions. I became more flexible and open, and I have achieved recognition that would not have come had I stayed the standard associate course. Now I feel confident to chase my dreams. And when I get to a fork in the road where I'm called upon to make a new decision, I now think, "Which way leads to more adventure?"

Ivy B. Grey is a legal tech entrepreneur, writer, and former practicing lawyer. Her work on technology competence, ethics, and innovation has made her a respected thought leader in legal tech. In 2018, Ivy was recognized as a Fastcase 50 Honoree and a part of the Women of Legal Tech by the ABA Legal Technology Resource Center. Ivy writes for *Above the Law* and *Law Technology Today*. She has spoken for multiple bar associations, the ABA TechShow, and several CLE providers.

Ivy is currently the director of business strategy for WordRake, an editing add-in for Microsoft Word. She is also the creator of American Legal Style for PerfectIt, a legal-specific proofreading add-in for Microsoft Word.

Ivy practiced corporate bankruptcy law for 10 years before making her transition to full-time legal tech in November 2018. During her decade of legal practice, Ivy was named a Rising Star in the New York Metropolitan

Area for five consecutive years, and her significant representations included *In re AMR Corp. (American Airlines), In re Dewey & LeBoeuf LLP, In re Eastman Kodak Company, In re Nortel Networks Inc.,* and *In re Filmed Entertainment Inc. (Columbia House).*

Ivy received her B.A. from Scripps College in Claremont, California; her J.D. from the University of Houston Law Center where she was chief Notes & Comments editor of the *Houston Business & Tax Law Journal*; and her LL.M. in corporate bankruptcy from St. John's University School of Law in Queens, New York. Prior to becoming a lawyer, Ivy worked in public relations and information technology. You can follow Ivy on twitter at @IvyBGrey.

Lesson 20

● ● ● ●

DREAM BEYOND PERFECTION!
MELANIE GRIFFIN

Perfectionism is self-destructive simply because there's no such thing as perfect.
Perfection is an unattainable goal.

— BRENÉ BROWN

My husband and I recently adopted a beautiful son. Wanting to be the best parents possible, the positives and negatives of our childhoods were analyzed. For me, the reflection revealed a main characteristic developed that deeply intertwined with my legal career—perfectionism. Although this attribute resulted in some pretty sweet successes – a silver lining – it also meant I was petrified of failure—a significant professional impediment.

To illuminate, during a conference addressing perfectionists' low self-esteem, decreased self-confidence, and minimalized achievements, a story was told about a female lawyer who let perfection overrun her practice. For years, she reviewed all of her office's work before it was finalized, the only way she could ensure perfection. Problematically, capacity limited her review capabilities, preventing her practice's growth. Additionally, the mounting documents required around-the-clock work to the exclusion of family and friends. The lawyer was unhappy both at work and home until eventually realizing that abandoning perfection would cause professional and personal growth. She committed that moving forward, at least 10% of her daily work would be "wrong," as dealing with the fallout from any associated mistakes was faster than perfection. The model was a success.

Like this lawyer, self-esteem, confidence, and failure issues often negatively impact female attorneys. To overcome such obstacles, women lawyers can use the following strategies to mentally reset to connect with the best within themselves.

Ask "how will," not "what if." For years, I constantly repeated all the ways I would fail. "What if I don't get into law school? What if no law firm hires me? What if I can't develop clients? What if my branch office is unprofitable?" What if, what if, what if…Despite my successful record making 100% failure unlikely, I never once challenged myself with a positive question like, "Melanie, how will you excel in law school? Serve as an effective associate? Provide impeccable client services? Motivate and empower others?" My singular focus was short-term negativity, not long-term goals or strategy. Thankfully, using the techniques herein, this mindset eventually shifted to planning for success and embracing failure, allowing me to find professional purpose, create a personal brand, expand my mentorship, and enjoy a newfound peace. So, the next time you start asking yourself, "*What if* I fail?" refocus on: *how will* you achieve your most audacious dreams?

Don't dwell. Learn and move forward. Like the "what ifs" early on, my mind was overrun with everything I wish I had done differently, that I wished had gone differently. Sadly, these alleged inadequacies oftentimes did not warrant the attention received, and rather, were trivial occurrences, such as a comment made at a party or a typo in an email that no one likely remembered but me. Despite the insignificance of these trivialities, they consumed my mind to the exclusion of forward-thinking thoughts worthy of my attention. Thankfully, a mentor stopped this negative habit by teaching me to learn from an imperfection by briefly recognizing how the moment could have been improved and then immediately moving on from it. Maya Angelou summarized this practice well when she reflected, "Do the best you can until you know better. Then when you know better, do better." Take her advice—when future imperfections surface, stay positive, focus on what you will do to change the outcome the next time, and smile knowing that due to the experience, you are now a better professional and friend.

Mentally practice positivity and goal achievement. Like physical exercise, mental positivity must be consistently practiced. Try the following techniques to build your mental prowess.

Learn through mentorship. My outlook changed upon attending women's empowerment programs. Learning from inspiring women, a key takeaway is keeping a physical object – a stuffed toy gremlin, for example – that represents your internal naysayer in your office. When leaving for important business matters, look at the "gremlin," say "goodbye," and physically depart from your internal self-doubt.

Focus through journaling and vision boarding. Consistent journaling, even if only for a few minutes each session, fosters goal achievement. For example, begin each workday by writing your daily goal, such as, "I am a great litigator." Or, "I inspire my attorneys to provide service excellence." These statements affirm what you *will* do, not what you *want* to do, which can breed self-doubt. Next, write what you *will* do that day to make your goal a reality. For example, a great litigator might draft her theory of a case to avoid litigating without a clear theme. Likewise, the firm leader inspiring service excellence might give each firm attorney a blank notecard to complete for a client.

Vision boarding images of your goals to hang in your office is similarly a good reminder of the dreams you *will* achieve. Two lawyer girlfriends annually co-host a party for local female attorneys to complete their boards together and cheerlead for each other. During the exercise, clip additional images to hang in your closet at home and on your bathroom mirror. Viewing these images over time opens your mind to the reality of big dreams that originally seemed unachievable.

Gain motivation from podcasts and audiobooks. Busy professionals have little time for non-work-related reading. You do, however, have time to listen, such as while driving or exercising, so replace your exhausted playlist with inspirational podcasts or audiobooks. To start, list five trailblazers from whom you want to learn. Search the podcast app for such names. The podcasts that scored such interviews are likely podcasts to which you want to consistently listen. Additionally, during their interviews, your heartthrob trailblazers will mention what inspires them. Add the referenced people and books to your list, and also review the related podcasts recommended by the app. My list is a note on my phone to easily personally reference and share with others. And, it is often used, as podcast and audiobook listening has afforded me tremendous growth, especially concerning the topics herein.

Embrace the awesomeness of failure. A recent podcast featured famed gymnast Nastia Liukin sharing that the singular standing ovation she received during her career was not after winning 2008 Olympic Gold, but after falling flat on her face at the 2012 Olympic Trials. Why? Because she got up and finished the competition despite knowing that her gymnastics career was over. She also connected with many others who believe that the worst possible outcome is failing to pursue your dreams, not "failing" to achieve them. Thus, when analyzing a new potential goal, consider if you'll regret someone else accomplishing it instead of you. If so, pursue it using the strategies herein to plan your "*how wills*" and silence your "*what ifs.*"

Additionally, change your definition of "failure." An outcome different than that originally envisioned is not "failure;" it's a chance to learn and grow on the best path for you. So, when things don't go as planned, take a deep breath, yell "plot twist!" and move on.

Be a dreamer, not a perfectionist. In sum, many women lawyers grow up believing perfection is the gold-standard. Oppositely, it oftentimes is unattainable, stagnates law practices, and precludes personal and professional growth. Thus, to find true happiness, forget the idealism breeding your fear of failure and unapologetically pursue what brings you true joy.

Melanie Griffin is a triple-graduate of The Florida State University (Business Finance, 2003; MBA, 2006; JD, 2006). Post-graduation, Melanie's entrepreneurial skills have been honed for thirteen years at the Dean Mead corporate law firm where she has served as a law clerk and then attorney since 2006, the last five years of which she was an equity shareholder and the managing partner of Dean Mead's Tampa office. Her leadership led to recognition as Florida's Most Productive Young Lawyer (2009); *Super Lawyers* Rising Star (Business Litigation 2010-19); *Florida Trend* Legal Elite (Up & Comer 2010-14; Commercial Litigation 2014-18); Best Lawyer in America (Commercial Litigation 2017-19); Tampa Bay Metro Inspiring Woman in Business (2016-17); TBBJ BusinessWoman of the Year Legal Services Finalist (2016); FSU Notable Nole (2016); and FSU College of Business Recent Alumni Achievement Award Winner (2017).

In 2017, Melanie created Spread Your Sunshine™, her personal brand and passion project through which she is focused on inspiring joy and building confidence in others. Melanie's success shining others beyond the glass ceiling was celebrated through her receipt of the 2016 *Tampa Bay Business Journal*

BusinessWoman of the Year Angie's Award, 2017 GSWCF Woman of Promise Award, 2017 FSU Inspire Award, 2018 Florida Bar YLD Outstanding Woman Lawyer of Achievement Award, 2018 KNOW Tampa feature, and 2019 The Best of KNOW feature. Melanie is happiest when she is building up all those around her, including her husband Mike, son Maverick, and Golden Lab Molly. Learn more about Melanie at www.spreadyoursunshine.com.

Lesson 21

● ● ● ●

MAKE YOUR ASK A GIVE
DEBBIE EPSTEIN HENRY

Every movement reveals us.

– MICHEL DE MONTAIGNE

Asking is uncomfortable. Many of you may be natural at developing relationships, but when it comes time to making an "ask" – whatever that ask may be – you fall short. Part of it may be a fear of failure that you ask for something that you don't deserve, or someone else deserves it more, or you can't deliver on it. It also may be a concern about jeopardizing relationships or trying to translate personal relationships into professional ones. Or, perhaps you are shy and not comfortable developing relationships in the first place, let alone making an ask for something that you want or need. Yet, not being able to ask – for that opportunity to represent a client, go on a pitch, or be considered for a job, promotion, leadership role or increased compensation – can impede your success. So how do you get there? Follow these tips and you should be on your way to mastering the art of the ask.

1. **Listen.** Before you ask anyone for anything, get to know them and their needs, interests, and challenges. The more you know, the greater your ability to help them.
2. **Make your ask a give**. By getting to know someone's needs and interests, you learn if what you can offer aligns with what they need. So, rather than frame your ask as a favor, see instead if you can offer to be a resource.

3. **Be generous.** Extend yourself. Whether it's taking someone out, sending them a relevant article, helping their child get a job or giving them advice, be there to help. It's much easier to ask when you're a giver. And, importantly, if you help someone, be sure it is not a quid pro quo. Instead, you should be helpful with no condition or expectation of a return.

4. **Be informative and inquisitive.** People need to know what you do so that you can be helpful to them and they can be helpful to you. Often social acquaintances are unaware of each other's jobs and interests. Let people know what you do and be inquisitive about what they do.

5. **Be visible.** Get involved. If you have visibility, you will be a natural resource to others. Provide advice and direction to people who seek you out for guidance. If you are available to address needs that your contacts have, you will likely be more comfortable asking for help in the future.

6. **Be a problem solver.** If you are a problem solver, people will come to you when they face challenges. Say "yes" to requests for calls and meetings. If you're not the one who can solve the problem, direct them to someone who can.

7. **Be a connecter.** It's important to share your network. If you know people who are amenable and can be helpful to your contacts, make those introductions. That said, when you facilitate introductions, remember that your contacts become an extension of you. Be sure that you are comfortable vouching for the people you recommend.

8. **Be worthy.** When you make an ask, be sure you are up to the task. Don't put anyone in a compromising position to advocate or create an opportunity for you. Also, once you make an ask, be sure to deliver. Be responsive, considerate, humble, and flexible in how you respond to someone who is willing to help.

9. **Blur professional and personal lines.** Making an ask of a friend or family member can be particularly hard. But social media is blurring the lines between professional and personal, and if you are unwilling to access your personal network, you will pay too high a professional cost. If you are making an ask of friends and family, focus on being generous as well as being a point-person, problem-solver, connecter, and overall resource. In most relationships, a natural reciprocity will ensue. As you continue to extend yourself, you will become more comfortable asking for help when you need it, too.

10. **Do your homework.** When you ask someone to do something on your behalf, be sure you've done the legwork in advance. You should know precisely what your ask is and how the person you're asking can be helpful.

11. **Make it easy.** If someone is doing you a favor, minimize the work for them. So, draft the email, have the resume ready to go, know the best point of contact, make the time and location convenient, and attend to any other details so the person you ask is only doing what you actually need them to do.

12. **Practice and role play.** If asking is hard for you, practice. Role playing can help you think through unanticipated issues and project more confidence when you make an ask.

13. **Make specific and small asks.** Build up your "ask tolerance" by starting with specific and small asks. This is a good way to test out a person's receptivity to assist. It will also get you more comfortable making bigger asks.

14. **Consider the venue.** Where you make an ask may determine the outcome. Be sure the person you are asking is in a comfortable place when you make your request. Also, be sensitive if anyone is witness to your ask in case someone else's presence would create an awkwardness.

15. **Watch your physical stance and tone.** Think critically about whether your ask should be made in person (which is typically preferable) or by phone or email. If in person, make eye contact and be thoughtful about having an open physical stance. How you frame your request and your tone of voice is important, too.

16. **Evaluate the timing.** A person's receptivity to an ask can vary based on when an ask is made. Time of day, week, month, or year may impact the response. These considerations should be factored in to maximize the likelihood of a yes.

17. **Ensure you have the right audience.** Be sure you are not making an ask of the wrong person. Also, make your ask personal and tailored. Take the time to address someone individually if you're asking that they do something on your behalf.

18. **Say "thank you."** Obvious right? But people often do not take the time to thank the people who have helped.

19. **Be prepared to ask again.** If you make an ask and the answer is "no," assume it means "not now." Ask the best way to follow up, the timing

and if there are others whom you should contact. Your ability to ask and the types of asks you make will change as your relationships evolve and deepen over time.

20. **Report back.** Follow-up with the people whom you asked, ideally with a personal note or call. Share with them the results of their efforts, what worked and who else was helpful to you.

If you are still reticent to make an ask after reviewing these tips, think about what will happen if you don't make the ask. Remember—the risk of inaction (not making an ask) is often greater than the ask contemplated.

Debbie Epstein Henry is an expert, consultant, best-selling author, and public speaker on careers, workplaces, women, and law. For 20 years, hundreds of news outlets have featured Debbie's work including *The New York Times*, *NBC Nightly News*, *The Wall Street Journal* and many more. She is the author of *Law and Reorder: Legal Industry Solutions for Restructure, Retention, Promotion & Work/Life Balance*, the #1 best-selling ABA Flagship book for 2011, and the co-author of another ABA best-selling Flagship book in 2015, *Finding Bliss: Innovative Legal Models for Happy Clients & Happy Lawyers*. Debbie conceived of the Best Law Firms for Women initiative, a national survey she developed with Working Mother and ran for a decade. By 2008, her visibility enabled her to build a national network of over 10,000 lawyers. From there, in 2011, she co-founded Bliss Lawyers, a company that employs high-caliber attorneys to work on temporary engagements for in-house legal department and law firm clients.

Debbie has received numerous awards including being named among the *Philadelphia Business Journal* "Women of Distinction." She is also the recipient of the Anne X. Alpern Award. Debbie volunteers her time with several nonprofits including the Forum of Executive Women where she is a member of the board and co-chair of the annual Leadership Symposium. Debbie is chair of Brooklyn Law School Women's Leadership Circle which runs a national women's law student and alumnae initiative. She received her B.A. from Yale University and her J.D., *cum laude*, from Brooklyn Law School. A native New Yorker, Debbie lives in the Philadelphia suburbs with her husband; they have three sons. Learn more about Debbie at www.debbieepsteinhenry.com.

Lesson 22

● ● ● ●

CHANGE THE WAY YOU CHANGE
THERESA A. HORTON

I went to the woods because I wished to live deliberately,
to front only the essential facts of life, and see if I could not
learn what it had to teach . . .
I left the woods for as good a reason as I went there . . . I learned this, at least,
by my experiment: that if one advances confidently in the direction of his dreams,
and endeavors to live the life which he has imagined, he will meet
with a success unexpected in common hours.

– HENRY DAVID THOREAU, FROM WALDEN

I offer here three mini-Lessons that work together powerfully and have helped me to craft a pleasing life.

TREAT YOUR LIFE AS AN EXPERIMENT.

For the first, I am indebted to Henry David Thoreau. His book *Walden* came out of an experiment Thoreau created to answer the question: On how little money, labor, and community can a person reasonably live? He undertook to find out by living with as much simplicity and solitude as possible for "two years and two months," and then went back to village life.

What a difference it makes if the cause of change is curiosity! It's so much better than "should" or "ought to" or worse, "have to." It doesn't matter whether these voices come from within or from outside, they still seem to deaden our joy.

Instead, ask a question. Here are a few examples:

- How would I feel if I didn't drink for a month?
- Would vigorous exercise really make me feel better?
- What would it be like to live without debt?

Create your own experiment and undertake it. See if you don't experience, as I did, much more ease in sticking to an experiment instead of a "permanent commitment." (How many New Year's resolutions have you broken?)

An experiment *has* to end so you can analyze it.

HONOR YOUR OWN SABBATH.

This idea of treating my life as an experiment led to experimenting with the second mini-Lesson, for which I am indebted to the Judeo-Christian tradition: Sabbath practice.

You need not be religious to engage in Sabbath practice. The key is cutting out distractions, media, any kind of aggressive behavior, and tasks that engage the left brain (like planning, accounting, analysis, and map-reading).

When I first decided to try Sabbath practice, I considered it quite daunting. If I gave up a whole day each week to rest and pursuits that were in no way tied to my self-interest, when would the housework, yardwork, and errands get done? I was dependent on having the whole weekend for those activities.

Or so I thought.

Instead, after a few nail-biting weekends, I relaxed into the practice, and *long* before the one-year experiment commitment had ended, I became convinced that this weekly interlude (setting aside goals, projects, tasks, distractions, hyperactive "recreation," and all commercial activity) is a powerful tool for effectiveness.

To put this in terms of pop neuroscience, Sabbath is a right-brain day. In terms of Jungian or archetypal psychology, Sabbath is feminine energy, and/ or a safe place for your Inner Child.

Tapping into that intuitive side supports creativity, opens the door to our unique individuality, and turns down the volume of our culture's propaganda so that we can hear our own true voice.

BE THE GATEKEEPER OF YOUR PALACE.

The third mini-Lesson came from self-observation as I tried to be consistent in my Sabbath practice. Some part of me had to "guard the gate" or "enforce the rules" like a sentry marching on the perimeter of the Queen's palace grounds.

My male energy, my inner parent, the rule-loving Pharisee in me was *serving* my feminine energy, the Sabbath Queen!

Imagine a loyal soldier protecting the Queen from intruders! This gives a role to the voice we were so happy to sidestep in the first mini-Lesson: the "should," "ought to," and "have to" voice. This image is especially heartwarming to me, as a woman. The Queen rules; the male energy simply protects her.

I learned that this "should" voice can be brought into play, not as an overlord, but as the *servant* of the more intuitive side. For example, it can help you to leave the office at a certain hour, whether you think you are finished with work or not. The Inner Parent is protecting the rest of your life and your other commitments.

Coming full circle, I found myself grateful for the gatekeeper, so long as he did not go rogue and try to usurp the Queen's place.

So, here are my three mini-Lessons:

1. Treat change as an experiment to see what you might learn or what works for you.
2. Experiment with "shut-down" time every single week to get in touch with your more intuitive side.
3. Give that bossy voice (and we *all* have one!) a task well suited to it.

Working together, these three mini-Lessons have given me the power to find inner harmony, to slow down, to initiate change at the office and at home when it was needed, and to deeply enjoy my life as it is.

By the way, this inner harmony – this lack of conflict inside – it's called integrity. And it feels wonderful!

A note on the quote: Thoreau was one of the freest thinkers in the history of American letters. He would never have limited his thoughts or observations to male humans only. When he was writing, use of the masculine pronoun was considered neuter and included all persons. I saw no reason to alter his beautiful language to mollify the sensitivities of the moment. I think he would approve.

Theresa A. Horton is a sole practitioner in Greenville, South Carolina, where she practices in the areas of probate, estate planning, and estate administration. Theresa earned her B.A., *with honors,* from the University of Florida in 1975 and her J.D. from the University of Texas at Austin in 1984. She has lectured in continuing legal education seminars for the South Carolina Bar and the National Business Institute since 1993.

Theresa indulges her creativity in writing, needlework (her original designs), cooking, interior design, and other collaborative endeavors with local artisans. Learn more about Theresa at www.theresahorton.com.

Lesson 23

● ● ● ●

BIG FISH, LITTLE POND
PEGGY HOYT

You have to do what you dream of doing, even while you're afraid.

—*Arianna Huffington*

I didn't start my legal career as an entrepreneur. I went to law school as a second career after spending approximately 10 years in the college recruiting, sales, and financial services industries. The primary thing I learned from that experience is I was never going to be a good "small fish in a big pond." I needed my own pond.

After law school graduation, I accepted an associate position with one of Orlando's larger law firms. It was a great place to learn about the law and the politics of working in a law firm. After three years, I was offered a position in a small all-woman law firm to head up its new estate planning department. I was thrilled but also terrified. There was no one in the firm that had estate planning experience that could mentor me.

I set out on a search for mentors. Naively, I believed small firm lawyers would be willing to help other small firm lawyers. I was wrong. However, I did meet one attorney who introduced me to a national estate planning organization that emphasized collegiality. The philosophy of the organization was if we all helped each other then we would all ultimately benefit from each other's experience and our practices would thrive. It was an "attitude of abundance" I have embraced since.

Eventually the day came when I reached a crossroad: Stay with the woman-owned firm or start my own firm. I had just read *Who Moved My Cheese,* and was inspired by the thought, "What would you do if you knew you would not fail?" I did a lot of soul searching, determined the worst that could happen was I would go bankrupt and humiliate myself. I held by breath and stepped out of a paycheck into the world of entrepreneurs. I have never looked back.

Making the decision to start my own law firm and create my own pond was one of the most profound and terrifying decisions of my life. Perhaps I was having a midlife crisis? I was 40 years old. I still didn't know what I wanted to be when I grew up. At an earlier time in my career I was turned down for a job based on five criteria: I was too young; I was over-educated; I had no experience; I was a woman; and I had blonde hair! Well, other than being too young, I probably still had all of those same challenges before me. My education had prepared me well for running a business and the practice of law. I had a degree in marketing and management, an M.B.A. in finance and a J.D. in law with a passion for estate planning. I had been in sales and had a successful four-year run as a financial advisor.

Still, I had no experience practicing law on my own or running my own business. I never had to rely solely on myself for the creation of my income and the success of a firm. Could I do it? That was the Mount Everest before me. I would always be a woman, and I still have blonde hair. Despite these perceived shortcomings, I embraced the challenge. I had been successful before. I could do it again.

However, I really didn't want to do it all alone. As the saying goes, "Misery loves company."

Fortunately, I had become friends with a colleague who also belonged to the collegial estate planning organization. He was 10 years younger, a U.S. Navy JAG officer, and with the encouragement of his spouse, decided he too was up for the adventure. He suggested I start out first, see how it went and then he would join me. Well, this is not exactly what I had in mind, but I took the leap anyway. I found some office space not too far from my home—after all, if I was going to have my own practice, I wasn't going to do the downtown commute. I "stole" my paralegal from my old firm so that day one I had a team that could help with running the office. I signed up with an employee leasing company and "leased" both myself and my paralegal so we would have access to benefits. I put both our salaries on a credit card and prayed—hard.

I have always been passionate about marketing. I like people. I love to network. I love to speak and teach. So, I did what every aspiring new business owner does: I got out there and met everyone I could, as fast as I could. This worked so well that I surprised myself. I was busy. I had clients. Yikes! The work was piling up and I didn't have enough energy at the end of the day to get it all done. At this point I was meeting with clients or influencers all day. That left the after-hours and weekends for doing the work, including at that time, all of the bookkeeping. I was exhausted and falling behind.

This was the time for my partner to make the leap, too! In the beginning I actually hired him to do the work I couldn't find the time to get done. In addition, he needed to build his clientele and used our "educate to motivate" model to introduce himself to prospective clients and to influencers who could send him more clients. In less than six months we agreed it was time to make our partnership official. Instead of two separate law firms, we consolidated our clients and our efforts to become one single law firm with a common goal: To provide outstanding service to families for estate planning and elder law.

Today, both my partner and I hold dual board certifications in estate planning and elder law. We have one non-equity partner and an associate. We have 10 support team members. We own our building and over the years we've served thousands of clients. Each member of the team brings a unique set of skills and a commitment to our shared values of honesty, kindness, and humanity.

Our law firm celebrated its 19th year in September 2018. My law partner and I have a true partnership relationship where all profits are shared equally. We have never measured our independent contributions to the firm; we have always respected that there will be times when one may contribute more than the other and then the tide will turn. Our common work ethic is the underpinning for the success of this approach. Also, we have always agreed to have consensus on an idea, or we will not do it. There have been times when we had to be patient in order to convince the other of a proposed suggestion, but that philosophy and approach has worked for us. By nature, I tend to be more of a risk taker, so my partner keeps me grounded. Likewise, I encourage him to take risks he might otherwise have avoided.

We created a firm built on a foundation of client education, lifelong relationships, and excellent service. All of our relationships begin with education—either an educational workshop or an educational consultation. We "teach our clients the questions they didn't even know they needed to ask." We have never stopped teaching; we hold numerous workshops monthly for prospective clients, existing clients, and the trusted advisor communities we serve. Each step in our process is designed to provide greater insight and clarity in a legal world where newcomers don't necessarily speak the language. We only work with people we like. This philosophy has given us the freedom to create our "perfect client."

We've created a firm culture we enjoy that reflects our personal values. We honor and respect our team. We treat them like family by acknowledging strengths and shortcomings in an atmosphere that rewards both growth and acceptance. In kind, our team treats our clients like family; we appreciate that without their respect and support, we don't have a place to work. We take checks, but we also take hugs. We don't always agree, but we always work it out. Each year gets a little bit better. We get older, while also getting wiser. I'm looking forward to another 19 years!

Peggy Hoyt is a Stetson University graduate receiving her B.B.A., *cum laude*, in 1981, her M.B.A. in 1982 and her J.D., *cum laude,* in 1993. Her work experience includes time as a college recruiter, financial consultant, account executive, and chief financial officer before entering law school. She is a founding partner of Hoyt & Bryan, LLC. Peggy is dual-certified by The Florida Bar in wills, trusts, and estates and elder law. Peggy practices in the areas of family wealth and legacy counselling, including trust and estate planning and administration, elder law, small business creation, succession and exit planning, real estate transactions, and animal law. In addition to her law degree, she holds a Florida real estate license. Peggy formerly held a NASD Series 7 license and health, life, and variable annuities licenses. She serves as a certified FINRA arbitrator and is also a Florida Circuit Court mediator concentrating in family business, estate administration, and animal law issues. Peggy also taught animal law as an adjunct professor with Barry University College of Law. Peggy speaks at the local, regional, and national levels on estate planning and elder law topics including pet planning, special needs planning, and planning for unmarried couples and same-sex partners. Peggy has been featured on *CNN Financial News* and in *The Wall Street Journal* and *the Orlando Sentinel* for her work in pet planning. Learn more about Peggy at www.hoytbryan.com.

Lesson 24

● ● ● ●

WHY SAYING YES MEANS SAYING NO

HEATHER HUBBARD

For every action, there is an equal and opposite reaction.

— SIR ISAAC NEWTON

Like many women, I was born and raised a people-pleaser. I wanted to be viewed as a hardworking and helpful team player, and I genuinely wanted to give back and serve others. I also had a deep burning desire to achieve as much as possible. Driven and ambitious, I never wanted to say no to an opportunity that might advance my academic or professional standing.

That means I said "yes" a lot. Looking back, it's hard to think of any requests or opportunities I turned down during the first decade of my legal career.

As could only be expected, I eventually began to suffer from burnout and exhaustion. When it got bad enough, I sought professional advice from coaches and counselors. During this time of wanting to do more but feeling completely exhausted, I learned an invaluable lesson—that every time I said "yes," I was also saying "no" to something or someone else.

Now this may sound obvious to you, but that was an earth-shattering concept for me.

As I tried to fully understand this principle, I kept thinking of Newton's third law of motion: "For every action, there is an equal and opposite reaction."

Yes, I was raising my hand. Yes, I was "leaning in." Yes, I was everything encouraged of young lawyers. And, yes, it paid off. I received promotions, awards, and financial gains.

But my personal life suffered in equal proportion. From my marriage to my physical health to my emotional well-being, it started to become painfully clear that I was paying dearly for the many areas of my life I had said "no" to over and over again.

For every "yes," there was indeed an equal and opposite "no." The trade-offs had finally caught up with me.

As I began to look more closely at my people-pleasing nature as well as my high-achievement drive, I realized it was going to be quite difficult for me to start setting boundaries and saying "no." What helped immensely was learning that I was already saying "no." For every "yes," there was an equal and opposite "no." Although this is now a leading principle in my life and something I rely upon to make decisions each and every day, it took some time to fully learn this lesson. To the extent you're where I used to be – struggling to say "no" – I'd like to share with you an example that might help.

Let's walk through a situation common to most lawyers: a networking event. Whether hosted by your firm, a bar association, community organization, or another company, there's an opportunity for you to attend an event. If you're anything like me, your first reaction might be, "I should be there." Perhaps you think it will look good or is expected of you. Maybe you're hopeful it will result in new business or a lucrative job lead. Or, possibly, you're just worried you'll miss out. Whatever the motivation, you think you should attend.

The only thing that crosses your mind is whether there's a conflict. You look at your calendar and you're free to go, so you RSVP with a resounding "yes." You don't even really think about it, you just say "YES!" When there's nothing on your calendar, it looks like blank space. You don't have anything else planned, so it doesn't seem as though you're saying "no" to anything else. There's no hard decision to be made. But that's not true, because it violates the law that for every "yes," there's an equal and opposite "no." There's always a trade-off, and that's where this Lesson can really change your life and career. I know it did mine.

Let's take a moment to consider what the trade-offs might be in this situation. What might you be saying "no" to? If you don't attend the networking event, what else might you do during this time? Would you stay at work and bill more hours or get caught up on non-billable administrative work? Would you exercise or spend time doing something you love? Would you go out on a date, meet up with friends, or have dinner with your family? The possibilities are endless, but you probably have an idea of the types of things you could be doing during this time if you didn't go to the event.

By saying "yes" to the networking event, you're effectively saying "no" to whatever else you could have been doing. I'm not suggesting that the networking event isn't something you should go to. You may very well decide that it is important, and you want to go. But the lesson I learned, and the one I hope will serve you just as well, is that you need to consider everything you're saying "no" to before you say "yes." Otherwise, you'll get in the habit of saying "no" to things that are actually more important than what you're saying "yes" to. When we reactively say "yes" without considering the opposite and equal reaction, we often find ourselves feeling overworked, overwhelmed, burned out, and unhappy. At least, that's what happened to me.

I now make it a point to stop and create space before I say "yes." Whenever I get an invite to attend a networking event (or a request to do anything else really), I make sure I'm thoughtfully responding instead of unconsciously reacting. I don't just look to my calendar to see if there's white space. Instead, I consider the many ways in which I could use that time, so I can choose the priority that's truly most important to me.

While we have a finite amount of time each day, we have infinite options on how to fill that time. This means we're constantly making choices, whether we realize it or not. Every single minute spent on one thing means it can't be spent on another. And every minute spent is indeed a choice.

Many times, I still say "yes" to the opportunity. Learning this lesson hasn't restricted my ability to say "yes." To the contrary. It now allows me to say "yes" (and "no") with more confidence. The more intentional I am with my time and priorities, the better I feel at the end of the day.

It has been very empowering to know that I can carefully weigh many wonderful options and then choose what's best for me. And while the ending might be obvious to you, I found the result to be a strange twist of fate. What I thought would require me to pull back and settle has helped me achieve even more success and happiness in my personal and professional career. It hasn't required me to make tough decisions; it simply required me to acknowledge that the decision is mine to make.

Heather Hubbard is the founder and president of All Rise LLC, a personal and professional development company supporting lawyers and law firms. Her weekly podcast, *Hustle & Flow with Heather Hubbard*, was recently named by the *ABA Journal* as one of the Top 25 legal podcasts in the country. Prior to establishing her own company, Heather was a partner and deputy practice group leader at an AmLaw 200 law firm. During that time,

Heather was recognized by *Best Lawyers in America* for Copyright, Trademark, Intellectual Property Litigation, and Patent Litigation. Heather has been recognized by *Mid-South Super Lawyers, Benchmark Litigation*, and has been named a Rising Star by *Managing IP*. She was also named one of Nashville's Top 40 under 40 by the *Nashville Business Journal*. Heather graduated *summa cum laude* from the University of Louisville and received her juris doctorate from Vanderbilt University Law School. Learn more about Heather at www.HeatherJoyHubbard.com.

This lesson was adapted from Hustle & Flow with Heather Hubbard podcast episode #8 originally released on March 28, 2017, with permission from All Rise LLC.

Lesson 25

●　●　●　●

GASLIGHTING AT WORK

ANNE KEVLIN

No one can make you feel inferior without your consent.

— *Eleanor Roosevelt*

I had never before asked anyone to give me a raise, but I was underpaid at my job as an attorney for a small insurance company. Not yet 30, I had three solid years of experience and had carried more than my weight, with good results. My boss was nice enough. I entered his office and made my case: I knew I had performed, and I knew that the going rate was $10,000 above my salary. What could be done to get me where I deserved to be?

My boss shook his head. "Anne, why is it that women are targeted by advertisers so much? Don't you find it offensive that young women feel the need to spend so much more money than men because of the way they are marketed to?" I probably looked as confused as I felt. "What do you mean?" I asked.

"I just don't think it is right that women feel like they have to shop so much that they go into debt," he said. "It must be so hard to be a woman in this society to feel compelled to spend, spend, spend." I was bewildered. My boss had deflected a reasonable request for a raise by suggesting that I spent too much money. Inaccurate premise notwithstanding, how an individual chooses to spend money has no bearing on whether she deserves a raise. I pointed this out to my boss's boss, along with actual salary data, all those years ago, and eventually got my raise, and a lasting career lesson.

So much is made of the theory that women's legal careers lag behind men's because women are fearful of asking for too much, lacking confidence in their own abilities, and underestimating their value to organizations. But even the strongest and most self-assured women may find their confidence rattled and their salary equity derailed by the particularly insidious work tactic of *gaslighting*.

Gaslighting is a sort of manipulation. It is a form of control, and it is abusive. The goal of gaslighters is to get their way by making the recipient question reality. Gaslighters distort the truth. The recipient may sense a misunderstanding at first, which may be cleared up. But a gaslighter will follow up with more efforts to confuse, withholding positive support and delegitimizing the recipient's needs, finding ways to criticize, addressing trivial events with righteous indignation, informing the employee that others have problems with the employee's work performance or behavior. The gaslighter will make him or herself out to be the true victim. Gaslighting tends to make an employee doubtful, anxious, and afraid. It may make her feel as if she can't do anything right. It may chill her from speaking up for herself. And it may go unidentified and be most destructive when a woman lacks confidence.

Gaslighting can occur when a manager feels threatened by a subordinate and wants her to leave her role; when a manager does not want questionable decisions to be challenged; or when a manager doesn't want to increase an employee's salary or promote her. I struggled in my twenties to distinguish gaslighting from truly productive negative feedback. Most work criticism is not gaslighting. Everyone has room to improve job performance, and appropriate negative feedback is valuable and necessary. My career has been blessed with many very good managers who have allowed me to respectfully and professionally seek details and ask questions about negative performance feedback, and who have supported my own efforts to improve.

Most people experience gaslighting in their careers, and this experience is not limited to junior attorneys. In a recent role, I led an in-house litigation team whose success meant that a significant and rapid expansion was in order. I was extremely proud. But as the hiring process was underway, my superiors – male non-attorneys – walled me off from communications about salaries for the new hires who would be reporting to me. This deviated from past practice. I was surprised, and offended, not to be included in what I felt were key considerations, not to mention professional courtesy and respect, for any leader.

I scheduled time with my boss. "I am concerned and confused that I am not being included in discussions about hiring and salaries for my team," I told him, calmly. His reaction was anything but calm. He glared. "I'm disappointed," he said. "You are just making this about yourself." Perplexed, I explained my position, but this only made him angrier. He brought up an unrelated email I had sent earlier in the week, apparently unhappy about it but never telling me why. He told me my discussion about salaries was wasting his time. I stayed calm, surprising even myself, flummoxed by his tone and the lack of reasonable explanation he provided for his reaction, equally sure that I was being neither unreasonable nor unprofessional. Eventually, my boss admitted that an offer had been accepted by an attorney who would be reporting to me, and that her salary would exceed my own by 10 percent. He then, oddly, asked me if I was upset. I lied and responded that I was not upset; I was fine. "No, you're not," he said, "I can tell you're not fine." His hostility was so out of character – until this encounter I had found him to be kind and reasonable – that I was left wondering how in the world I had ruined our professional relationship in less than 20 minutes.

I have learned that when performance criticisms are vague and general, or based on feedback from unnamed sources; if efforts to clarify or learn more about the criticized behavior are met with hostility or impatience; if the criticism seems simply wrong, unreasonably harsh, or irrational – a professional and polite email that is cited as being offensive, for example – those things may well be gaslighting.

And gaslighting may be one reason that women fall behind men in career promotions and pay. Women who accept gaslighting as legitimate feedback, incorrectly blaming themselves for their failure to advance, may never advance, may never get a fair salary increase, and may never view themselves as capable of succeeding in a new role or with a new boss. It is easy to see how women who want to please their bosses unwittingly hurt their careers.

Especially for women, confidence can be elusive. By focusing on what others think about us, rather than our own sense of right and wrong, good and bad, and what works for the paths that we choose for ourselves, we lose our own view of what we bring to the table. Women should instead focus on the successes and achievements we have accomplished in our careers, and the lessons we have learned when things didn't go according to plan. Trusted superiors, peers, mentors, or friends and family members who do not work with us, may be the best judge of what is fair criticism and what is inappropriate gaslighting.

Worrying about approval from others also prevents women from taking confidence-building risks. Avoiding failure by avoiding risks is no way to build confidence. Failure is a part of everyone's life. Overcoming defeat – learning from mistakes, surviving humiliations, and then finally getting back on our feet – leads to greater confidence and strength, which insulates us from gaslighting.

Having a growth mindset also helps women resist the negativity of gaslighting. A *fixed* mindset assumes we have innate abilities and inabilities that can never change. A *growth* mindset assumes that we can learn and become skilled in any area. It may take time and effort, but we can learn to be good at calculus, or golf, or tax law. We know that any skills we lack are skills we can acquire. Criticisms become challenges.

Ultimately, the way around gaslighting most often is to leave the employment situation that fosters it, particularly when the problem involves career progression or salary. That is what I did when efforts at reasonable salary discussions were met with hostility. Women need to move away from the harmful impact of gaslighting by taking steps to prove our detractors wrong. Over time, the inability to reason with or please gaslighters will chisel away at self-esteem, will waste valuable energy, will lead to undue stress or health issues, and will keep us from achieving parity with men.

My Lesson: Learn to recognize gaslighting, learn to ignore gaslighting, and learn to maneuver your career away from gaslighting.

Anne Kevlin has more than 25 years of insurance litigation and regulatory experience attained through private law practice as well as in-house roles with insurance entities. Anne began her law career in Florida, defending workers' compensation insurance matters. She later held in-house litigation roles in Minneapolis with SFM and The Hartford, followed by litigation management and regulatory compliance roles with The Hartford and First State Management Group in Boston, and Beazley, a global Lloyd's managing agent. Anne has developed and led a litigation department at a Florida homeowner insurer, and recently became managing partner for a national insurance defense law firm. She is a frequent presenter on insurance law and litigation management. Anne obtained her law degree from the University of Iowa, and her Master's in management from Harvard's Extension School. She has also completed her CII Award in London Market certificate.

Lesson 26

● ● ● ●

PRACTICAL ESSENTIALS FOR PROFESSIONAL SUCCESS: KNOWLEDGE – TRUST – SOLUTIONS

DEVIKA KEWALRAMANI

If you are passionate enough, push hard enough, want it enough,
success is already yours.

– *NOMBINI KUTTA-MATHYE*

Not so long ago, for a woman to become a lawyer was perceived by many as a symbol of success. Today, successful women lawyers are redefining professional achievement and transforming the future of lawyering. But how does the legal profession and society measure success? What can we do to sustain success? And, how do we know if we are successful at all? I think that success is what happens when women lawyers seek out and create their own unique opportunities in a way that feels right for them. We can set our individual sights and reach our professional heights—that is the modern woman lawyer's mantra for success. It is that freedom to make professional choices that makes success as a woman lawyer so poignant.

In my professional experience, three essential ingredients – knowledge, trust, and solutions – have helped to shape my law practice as I grew my client relationships, cultivated my professional network, and built my credentials. These elements are the pillars on which professional success stands steady, regardless of the setting of your practice or stage of your career—whether you are outside or in-house counsel, in public interest or the government, at a large, midsize or small firm, or a newly-admitted or an experienced lawyer. Ask yourself these questions: Are you sufficiently knowledgeable about your subject matter and able to handle difficult issues for clients? Have you built a circle of trust so that clients feel comfortable that they can rely on your judgment and advice? Do you offer practical solutions to resolve client problems?

GAIN KNOWLEDGE – BE A RESOURCE – DEVELOP A REPUTATION.

My practice involves advising other lawyers and law firms on legal ethics and defending them in disciplinary and admissions matters. It is a dynamic and evolving area that is complex and nuanced, requiring constant study, review, and analysis. Although having in-depth knowledge about the rubric of laws, rules, and cases in your area of practice is undoubtedly important, it is your wider understanding of their impact on your client's business or interests that makes you an asset when the phone rings and it is your client calling with an urgent or sensitive matter that requires careful and prompt resolution. Clients value having a "go-to" resource whose instinct, judgment, and experience they can rely on, even if they may be picking their lawyer's brain on issues having nothing to do with their particular matter. Being there and making yourself available can mean everything to clients. Years later, they may not remember why they called you, but they will never forget how you "dropped everything" to help them.

As you start building your reputation in a particular practice or niche, you will become increasingly visible to your colleagues, clients, and peers who will begin to turn to you as the point person for a specific type of issue or matter. This may feel very satisfying because you are being recognized as someone who is capable in your field of practice. These interactions may lead to other opportunities for advancement, whether internal or external, where you may be selected for significant or high-level assignments, cross-marketing initiatives, key appointments to professional panels or prestigious advisory boards, invited to speaking engagements, and asked to co-author articles in leading legal or trade publications.

I cannot emphasize enough the significant contributions we can make to our profession through active participation or leadership roles in bar association committees or other professional organizations. Early in my career, I became involved with bar association committee projects and later on, I took on various leadership roles where I had the opportunity to work closely with other committee members on emerging legal developments that would soon remodel certain aspects of my area of practice. This afforded me greater access to professional colleagues who would otherwise be outside my reach. Outside professional activities that are related or even unrelated to one's law practice have the potential to open up many doors for women lawyers that may not be so easy to unlock unless one gets out there: networking and collaboration opportunities, entrée to professional relationships, and even key introductions and business generation.

BUILD TRUST AND CREATE CONFIDENCE IN YOUR ABILITIES.

A client's trust is a lawyer's gift. But first, we need to learn to trust in ourselves—the abilities we have, the skills we have honed, and the advice that we give. Similarly, clients must feel comfortable knowing that they are in good hands. Trust and confidence take time to build. It took me time to begin to believe in myself, the work I am capable of doing, and what it is I have to offer to clients. As I gained experience with more complex client matters, my comfort level grew. But client trust can be a very delicate thing. As lawyers, we need to keep re-establishing trust and proving to ourselves and to our clients that we are worthy of their trust. How do we do that? Start with a few simple things:

- Always be available to assist
- Do excellent work
- Offer clients realistic advice
- Show an interest in their business and activities

These are a few easy ways to stay connected with clients and to ensure that they know you are there for them every step of the way.

FIND PRACTICAL SOLUTIONS. THAT'S WHY THE CLIENT CALLED "YOU."

It's no secret that a satisfied client is someone who you helped solve a problem, however big or small. Doing it quickly and effectively is a plus. It is our responsibility to be able to understand the client's needs and objectives, spot the issues that could interfere with the client's goals, and find a practical way for the client to pursue his or her interests. I learned early on that to be a successful lawyer one must listen very carefully to what the client is saying, ask intelligent questions, keep the client's needs in mind throughout, and then try to come up with the best possible solution under the circumstances. Finding a solution may not always be simple, but being solution-oriented is key. Clients value lawyers who can look at issues strategically, with a focus on reaching sensible and viable solutions for them.

Devika Kewalramani is a partner and co-chair of Moses & Singer LLP's Legal Ethics & Law Firm Practice which advises other law firms, lawyers, and legal departments on ethical and legal aspects of lawyering. She is also the firm's general counsel. Devika focuses on legal ethics, professional discipline, law firm risk management, lawyer licensing, and admissions matters. She conducts ethics and risk management audits for clients.

Devika is co-chair of the Council on the Profession of the New York City Bar Association, a member of its Committee on Professional Ethics, and the immediate past chair of its Committee on Professional Discipline. She was appointed a member of the New York Commission on Statewide Attorney Discipline in 2015 and served as co-chair of its Subcommittee on Transparency and Access. Devika is a member of the Advisory Board of the Ethics Institute of the New York County Lawyers' Association, the Foundation Board of The City University of New York School of Law, and the Editorial Board of the Practical Lawyer published by ALI CLE.

A frequent lecturer, panelist, and author, Devika speaks to law firms, legal departments, bar associations, and other professional groups on legal ethics. She is the author of Lexis Practice Advisor® for Corporate Counsel: Ethics for In-House Counsel. Devika served as a rules editor for *The New York Rules of Professional Conduct* (2010-2012), published by Oxford University Press, edited by the Ethics Institute of the New York County Lawyers' Association. She achieved Super Lawyer status in the Metro Edition of *New York Super Lawyers*® (2014-2018). Learn more about Devika at www.mosessinger.com.

Lesson 27

● ● ● ●

BUILD YOUR NEST

NELLY N. KHOUZAM

Little by little, the bird makes its nest.

— *FRENCH PROVERB*

In 2017, I was honored to give a commencement address to a group of law students. I wanted to offer them meaningful, valuable, and practical suggestions as they embarked on their legal careers. So, when I was invited to write a Lesson for this book, I decided to expand on those remarks and tailor them to my new audience. I want to make clear at the outset (and not to disappoint the readers) that I do not have a magic formula that applies just to women; rather, my suggestions apply to both men and women.

Each of you already has achieved so much and overcome many obstacles in your legal careers. And despite the lawyer jokes you may hear, you are members of what I believe to be the most noble of professions. A lawyer is an advocate, a counselor. That is, a lawyer is someone who assists individuals with their problems. Yet, it is important to remember that a legal career is not built overnight; rather, it is built over time and on day-to-day actions. There is a French proverb, "Petit a petit, l'oiseau fait son nid." It is a charming little phrase that is widely applied and translated as, "Little by little, the bird makes its nest." Like the little bird, you need to patiently build your nest.

This proverb speaks to the importance of a having good reputation, which undoubtedly includes hard work, patience, and perseverance. I consider reputation to be the most important aspect of an attorney's career because it can make or break you. It really does not matter if you are brilliant or are a great orator/speaker/oral advocate. If you have a reputation for being untrustworthy, you will have a very difficult time in your practice. You have probably heard this saying, "Do right, and you forget it. Do wrong, and you never forget it." It is true!

For example, I still remember an incident that happened to me over 35 years ago when I was a young lawyer. At a hearing in a civil matter, my opposing attorney, who was considerably older and had been in practice for decades, cited to a nonexistent statute. The judge, recognizing astutely that he "was trying to pull a fast one," chided my opponent for attempting to mislead the court. Unfortunately, to this day, the opposing attorney's reputation has never recovered. So never forget that, like the little bird in the proverb, you are building a nest, piece by piece.

HOW TO BUILD YOUR NEST

Work hard. No matter how smart you are, there is no substitute for preparation. Your commitment and dedication to hard work and investment in knowledge is the key to success. Do your homework, research the issue, and take the time to prepare. It is very evident to judges and employers whether someone has or has not fully prepared a given task. Again, you do not want to have the reputation of one who just "wings it" and is not thoroughly prepared.

Be punctual. Always remember to be on time. I recall fondly my senior partner in my private practice days who was always early for depositions, hearings, and trials. He factored in time for traffic and was always on time. He specifically told me to never have the reputation of being late as people will always talk about you. He was right. When I was on the circuit court bench and rotated to the criminal division, even before handling my first docket, I was warned by my colleagues about one particular attorney's tardiness. It is never good to be remembered in this manner by judges. Be on time and you will never have to worry.

Be a zealous advocate, but keep in mind that it is important to remain humble. Never seek the limelight. We all know members of the Bar who are always trying to impress others by showing off and bragging about their accomplishments. Resist that temptation. Let your actions speak for themselves.

Finally, be professional. Though we hear it all the time, what does this actually mean? Professionalism is all about how you conduct yourself in your dealings with others. If someone asks you for an extension of time to respond to your complaint, give it to him or her. It means taking a deposition in a civilized manner. It means taking the high road, regardless of the bird-brained way your opponent may handle himself or herself. It means conducting yourself in a manner that your mother, father, or partner would be proud of!

So where does that leave you? What does this mean to each of you? It means, keep building your nest. Work hard, be punctual, be patient, be professional, and stay humble in whatever area of practice you are in. So long as you keep your focus on building your nest, you will persevere and shine. You never know, maybe someday you will be the one sharing your nest-building lessons with an audience of attorneys.

Appellate Court Judge Nelly N. Khouzam is a "Double Gator" who attended the University of Florida as an undergraduate, and then graduated, *with honors,* from the University of Florida College of Law in 1981. She currently serves as an appellate court judge on the Second District Court of Appeal in Florida. As an AV-rated lawyer, she was a shareholder at Fowler, White, Gillen, Boggs, Villareal and Banker, P.A., and later at Silberman and Khouzam, P.A. Prior to joining the Second District Court of Appeal in 2008, she served for 14 years as a circuit court judge in Florida's Sixth Judicial Circuit.

A frequent author and lecturer, Judge Khouzam has written articles for *The Florida Bar Journal, Nova Law Review, Litigation Magazine,* and the *Trial Advocate Quarterly.* She is a frequent lecturer at judicial conferences and is a faculty member of the Florida Appellate and New Judges College. She is a past chair of the Florida Conference of Circuit Judges.

Judge Khouzam has received numerous awards, including: the A.B.O.T.A. "Florida Jurist of the Year Award" (2002); the William Castagna Award for Judicial Excellence for displaying the highest standards of judicial excellence in knowledge of the law, ethics, civility, professionalism, and demeanor (2006); and the John U. Bird Distinguished Jurist Award presented by the Clearwater Bar Association in recognition of extraordinary service as a trial and appellate Judge (2008). She has been a member of the American Board of Trial Advocates (A.B.O.T.A.) since 1993 and is past president of the Barney Masterson Inn of Court. She is a member of the American Law Institute, the nation's most respected and influential organization working to clarify and improve the law.

Lesson 28

● ● ● ●

BECOMING VISIBLE

RENEE NEWMAN KNAKE

For men and women, the first step in getting power is to become visible to others, and then to put on an impressive show.

— SANDRA DAY O'CONNOR

This Lesson is about visibility—what we see, being seen, and what we do.

WHAT WE SEE

As a law student walking to classes through the echoing glass and concrete halls of the University of Chicago Law School, I regularly passed the larger-than-life portrait of a grey-haired, stern looking woman in a light purple suit. She was the only woman on a wall of men. She also was the only woman on the faculty for many years, but I didn't know that at the time. I saw the portrait, but I didn't see myself in her.

Fast forward 10 years. As a law professor conducting research on women considered for the United States Supreme Court, I uncovered the stories of nine women shortlisted before Sandra Day O'Connor became the first female justice. One is Soia Mentschikoff, the only woman to appear on President Lyndon Johnson's shortlist for the United States Supreme Court, the second woman ever to appear on such a list. She was the first female law professor at Harvard University and the University of Chicago at a time when most law schools did not even admit women law students, let alone hire them as faculty. She became the University of Miami Law School's first permanent female dean. It was her portrait I'd walked by as a student.

What we see matters. It is nearly impossible to envision ourselves in a position of leadership or power if we do not see others in the role with whom we can identify. As Madeline Albright noted in more than one speech, "I never imagined that I would one day become secretary of state. It's not that I lacked ambition. It is just that I had never seen a secretary of state in a skirt."

This makes what women like Mentschikoff did so extraordinary. At the time, no woman had held the positions she would attain over the course of her career. But, she made herself visible so that she and others could rise within the legal profession.

BEING SEEN

I never had the good fortune to meet Mentschikoff in person. She passed away in 1984; I was just nine years old. Yet, over the course of my career in the legal academy, Mentschikoff has gone from a painting on the wall to a mentor in my personal and professional life. As women, we are often told that to 'get ahead' we should find a mentor. I struggled with that early in my career, in part because it was difficult to find someone willing to reveal the complexities of navigating one's personal and professional life in a vulnerable and honest way. This isn't surprising given that in order to advance in the profession, women often suppress the desire to speak out about disadvantages for fear that doing so might cause some sort of retaliation. We pump breast milk in cramped airplane bathrooms, we do the same (or more) work for less pay, and we endure gawking and groping in order to get through the day.

No one told me I might find a mentor by getting to know a dead woman. But as I rolled up my sleeves and dug through Mentschikoff's personal papers in the University of Chicago's Regenstein Library, I felt a kindred spirit, a bond. I held the index cards she meticulously prepared before teaching each of her courses. I read news articles describing what she wore to work (frivolous hats with eye-length veils) and how much she spent annually from her $2,800 lawyer salary in 1940 ($130 for cigarettes and liquor, $350 on clothing, $20 on books). I learned about her love affair with the prominent legal scholar Karl Llewellyn, sparked while she worked at a desk placed in his office at Columbia Law School when both served as reporters for the *American Law Institute's* Uniform Commercial Code project, that would evolve into a 16-year marriage ending at his death. She inspired me, and mentored me, as have other shortlisted women in my research. (You can read all about them in *Shortlisted: Women, Diversity and the Supreme Court,* forthcoming NYU Press, written with my wonderful friend and colleague Professor Hannah Brenner.) The most important lesson I learned from Mentschikoff is the power of seeing and being seen.

WHAT WE DO

Becoming visible is difficult in and of itself. I raised my hand only once during my three years in law school and never spoke during faculty meetings as a junior academic. But as I was 'mentored' by Mentschikoff and the other women in my research, I realized the importance of being seen and also being heard. I began to speak up. When the former dean of the school where I worked at the time advised me to avoid the tenure-track because my then-husband had "a good job" at the university and "pursuing tenure is stressful," I told the current dean I wanted a tenure-stream position and worked hard to earn the faculty votes for promotion. Soon after, I was called the "Norma Rae of the faculty" when I pointed out that entry-level women were paid less than their male counterparts. Keep in mind this was in the early 2000s—not the early 1900s. My scholarly expertise originally focused on legal ethics, but now a significant part of my work is devoted to remedying the remaining gender inequities.

Remembering the stories of women like Mentschikoff, who made themselves visible at a time when women were not seen, can inspire all of us to continue their work toward a legal profession led by individuals who reflect the public we serve.

Renee Newman Knake serves as Professor of Law and the Doherty Chair in Legal Ethics at the University of Houston Law Center. Prior to joining Houston Law in 2016, she served as the Foster Swift Professor of Legal Ethics and co-director of the Kelley Institute of Ethics and the Legal Profession at Michigan State University, where she taught for a decade. There, she founded the school's inaugural law laboratory to inspire entrepreneurship and innovation in legal services, recognized as a top program in the nation.

Renee held the Fulbright Distinguished Chair in Entrepreneurship and Innovation at Royal Melbourne Institute of Technology in 2019, and also has been a visiting scholar at Stanford Law School's Center on the Legal Profession and the American Bar Foundation. Her award-winning publications (four books and over 20 articles) have been cited in prestigious law reviews such as the *Yale Law Journal* and a range of media including *Bloomberg Law*,

The Christian Science Monitor, CNN Money, The Houston Chronicle, National Public Radio, The New York Times, and *The Wall Street Journal.*

Renee is an elected member of the American Law Institute and was appointed as reporter for the American Bar Association Presidential Commission on the Future of Legal Services. She also served as a delegate to the World Economic Form Global Agenda Councils on Justice and Rule of Law. Before her academic career, Renee practiced law at Mayer Brown, Hunton & Williams, and the Charlottesville, Virginia City Attorney's Office. She earned her J.D. from the University of Chicago Law School. Learn more about Renee at www.reneeknake.com.

Lesson 29

● ● ● ●

THE PEARL NECKLACE
KATE KYRES

A life lived in fear is a life half-lived.

— BAZ LUHRMANN

We are born with the potential to create our own pearl necklaces. Our pearls begin to form as we move through life experiences. When an oyster's solitude is invaded – say by a grain of sand – it responds to the invader by secreting nacre, a light but incredibly strong mother-of-pearl substance. Over the years, the oyster diligently secretes its powerful nacre, layer upon layer, until a pearl is formed—one pearl unlike any other created in nature.

As meaningful life experiences invade our solitude, we too shape our pearls. Some enter college with nascent strands. When I entered a private women's college, my irregularly shaped pearls were layered with nacre.

In the summer of 1977, I turned thirteen. At that time, domestic violence and child abuse laws were not meaningfully written or enforced. A summer evening encounter with a police officer created the most luminescent pearl on my strand when I witnessed the perverse allocation of power. I watched my mother beg for help while my older brother sat in a fetal position, faceless and motionless. Instead of the officer offering us protection, he shamed my mother for working late and for not being home to prevent her husband from "snapping." In disbelief, I asked him if he had a daughter to which he replied, "Yes." I implored him to remember my face when he looked at her. I told him that I wanted him to *see me*.

At thirteen, *I saw me*; a funny, smart girl who had power and right to lay claim to a beautiful life. Despite many terrifying times, my mother's intelligence, courage, and resourcefulness saved our lives. The pearls laid upon her breasts illuminated my path to college.

I hesitated to pursue a law degree after graduation from college. One of my pearls needed time secreting layers of nacre defending against the specter of a professor who I had encountered my junior year abroad while studying art history in Florence. He wrote a letter to me saying that I was not smart enough to grasp the theoretical concepts inherent in the practice of law so I should never go to law school. I ripped up that letter. My pearl necklace continued to grow.

I loved law school. The opportunity to dabble in different, complex legal studies without concern for life application to a distressed family, imprisoned person, or bankrupting company was explosively exciting. I loved to feel the weight of societal strife argued by passionate lawyers in legions of paper bound in heavy leather treatises.

The watershed times in my youth were fortunately an amalgamation of love, humor, and strife. Humor has always been my preferred nacre. From humor can flow love, compassion, and hope. Humor can disarm. Humor can connect our humanity. Humor served me well in law practice. I always searched for the humorous storytellers; the perplexed thinkers; the vibrant lovers and protectors of life and liberty. The practice of law is loaded with these creatives. They clang their pearls wherever they roam. Find these lawyers and collaborate with them.

One of my pearls was shaped during my first appeal. I was working for a firm that gave me incredible opportunities to layer my pearls. Right out of law school, I was provided a leather chair, a big desk with an intercom to beckon my assistant, and an unspoiled view of Tampa Bay. I had made it, and my first state court appeal and oral argument had me pinching myself. I represented a white mother who remarried a black man and, who, to this day I believe, lost primary residential custody of her daughter because of her interracial remarriage. My client pursued an appeal to build up the pearls of her necklace for her daughter. The case involved complex constitutional issues. We didn't win. But the experience of representing this strong woman shaped one of my irregular pearls into a strong, round one.

Another one of my pearls was shaped by a disabled father's harassment case. Every day on the job, he was mocked. After work, he returned home to care for his disabled child. During a full day of depositions, he listened to each one of his coworkers' and supervisors' sworn testimony that they didn't recall hearing anything said about his disability. Then the final witness walked in. He testified that he had heard every alleged harassing comment, every day, multiple times a day, coming out of the hateful mouths of all the men who had just testified that they didn't recall a word of it. When my client and I went to our cars, he cried.

There were many pearl-shaping moments in my discrimination law practice. My law office was broken into, glass smashed, nothing stolen, but a plant was ceremoniously placed in the center of my foyer's floor. I appeared before judges who applied dissimilar standards of diligence to counsel standing before them. I experienced bullying beyond mere posturing and several scary threats made by defendants. During my first deposition as a new lawyer, I was dispatched to observe a case involving many lawyers. A meddlesome attorney seated next to me asked if my briefcase was made from penile foreskin. I told him to shut up. Today, I would stroke my pearls and offer a fitting retort.

I had many professional successes in my practice. Nacre made my pearls grow rounder and more lustrous. But the pearl that I could not live my life without having was being a nurturer to my own child. When you represent clients in pregnancy discrimination cases and you secretly cry alone in your law office's bathroom for hours while miscarrying for a third time, you clutch your pearl necklace to your heart, and you reflect on your pearls.

I became a mother through adoption and concomitantly, a life trustee of a beautiful daughter. She is the most important case that I have ever worked on. I am all in—just like I was in my law practice. I am her mom, building my pearls which she will one day have. So, for a season I left the orbit of law and entered a new one designed to shape both of our necklaces. I created a children's business and have self-published the first of – hopefully – many children's books based upon stories that I always carry around in my pocket. This orbit and the legal one circle one another in harmony, and their co-existence will allow me to fly between the two when I so choose. I am a lawyer for life.

You see, the polestar lesson, truth, and value of being a lawyer is that your profession and your role in that profession have no shelf life. You can practice to the degree of your choosing when you are mindful of the type of advocate that your pearl necklace inspires you to be. Wear your pearl necklace proudly, and don't hesitate to clang it.

Kate Kyres is the creator of Silly Dilly's at The Enchanted Spot. The Kindness Kitty is the concierge of her vintage-inspired storybook shop. The

Kindful Mouse is the concierge of her educationally, entertaining event Parlor and the protagonist barrister in her Kindful Mouse Social Intelligence Workshop where she helps children explore their behavioral capacities through the use of literary, philosophical, and legal principles.

Kate studied behavioral traits in friendly mice at Simmons College while obtaining her degree in psychology. She studied art history and political theory as well. For a few years, she delighted in working with renovators of Boston brownstones which fueled her passion for designing her own furniture and nests. She enjoyed the challenge of practicing discrimination law and relished authoring a significant whistleblower law amicus brief while she served as president of the Florida Chapter of the National Employment Lawyers Association.

Her love of editing a local bar magazine with law gal pals influenced her writing dreams which today are realized in her published and forthcoming children's books. Kate recently created The Rainbow Swan which serves as the concierge of her Broadroom, a broad concept workroom for her events and for other women creatives to play. She dispenses legal and life advice to women on career, family, and life matters through Broadroom Consulting. She loved being a law student at New England Law and misses her big "editor in chief" swivel chair in the law review office. Good times there helped her graduate *magna cum laude*. Learn more about Kate at www.sillydillys.com.

Lesson 30

● ● ● ●

FOLLOW YOUR BLISS

BARBARA LEACH

Follow your bliss and the universe will open doors for you where
there were only walls.

— *Joseph Campbell*

Follow your bliss," says Joseph Campbell. Three years into lawyering, I thought, "What does he know?" I was working ungodly hours, wallowing in the fact that even after three years, I knew nothing, and I couldn't see an end in sight. So, I did just that: I ended it. Armed with $20,000 cash stored in my sock drawer and the conviction that I could "figure it out," I quit the practice of law. I didn't know who I was, but I knew I didn't want to be a lawyer.

That resolve lasted an entire 10 days. Upon learning I had left "The Practice," my girlfriend asked if I was interested in doing some hearing coverage for her. Another girlfriend wanted me to serve as an *ad hoc* associate on a $10 million case. I had nothing but time and a desire to help my friends, so I was all in.

Over the next six months working with these brilliant women, I realized maybe it wasn't the *practice* of law that left me bliss-less; maybe it was the fact I was practicing in a *law firm*. More specifically, a law firm that, while doing good, sophisticated work for its large, institutional clients, was a firm that practiced a sterile law, one that removed me from helping folks on an individual, personal basis.

Out of this soul-searching was born Barbara Leach Law, PL, affectionately BleachLaw because, well, we clean up your messes. Why am I sharing the origins of BleachLaw with you? The closest I came to "my bliss" during my first three years was the time I spent hanging out with my legal girlfriends, through our mutual membership in the Central Florida Association for Women Lawyers. It was the vehicle through which I met kindred spirits: other lawyers who were questioning what they were doing with their professional lives; other lawyers who were striking out on their own, boldly following their own individual definitions of bliss-filled existences; and other lawyers who had established themselves as role models to us and reveling in their successes.

I want you, gentle reader, to know that after I finally took the time to ask myself the deep questions – Do I even want to practice law? What do I want a practice to look like? Can I be soul-satisfied as a lawyer? – I have been infinitely pleased with the result. Walking into our boutique family and bankruptcy law firm is like walking into my living room. We don't want to be like other law firms. We want our clients to know we care about them from the first moment. Heck, we even have a firm mascot, Brulee, the long-haired Chihuahua, more affectionately known as the ChiLAWhua, who greets clients and colleagues from her perch on my desk.

It's been almost eight years since I "gave up law," and I'm super glad I did. I didn't give up the practice of law; I gave up others' expectations of what the practice should be. I love that I get to call the shots and work with clients I want to work with. And I really love that I get to work with the people with whom I want to work. My paralegal Marisela has been putting up with me for almost seven years, and even though I exasperate her on a daily basis with my ADHD-like desire to multitask and get involved in plenty of non-billable volunteer opportunities, she is the first one to say we have fun in our office.

I'm doing everything I can to show Stephanie, our two-year attorney who has been with us since getting admitted to the Bar, that she can forge the path she wants as a lawyer. (This is particularly easier for her because she's smarter than I ever was.) I want her (and you) to never feel alone, to know that there are others who are feeling exactly as you are or have felt that way previously. Right now, there are women (maybe reading this Lesson) who are on the fence about giving up law, feeling confined, constricted by someone else's expectations of the clients to serve, the law to practice, the firm to emulate. There are women who are worried about if they were to seek their own bliss, how that bliss might differ stridently from what others' expectations are.

My suggestion? Get yourself a band of cheerleaders. Open yourself to the possibility that you're seeking more, and surround yourself with supporters who will compel you to crystalize and realize your vision. When I was conceiving of BleachLaw, I had a "kitchen cabinet" of successful women lawyers who gave me feedback on all aspects of my future firm: logos, name, website address, firm color (yes, that's a thing). While ultimately these were my decisions to make, I felt emboldened in my choices because I had such fans alongside me in the process. You, too, can have that if you want. And for that matter, if you don't think you have sufficient members of your fan club, count me in!

The more I practice and hone what is the bliss I seek, the more I realize part of that is motivating and inspiring lawyers to take the leap that I did all those years ago. I spend a good amount of volunteer time teaching lawyers how to improve their practices through technology. I never imagined that would be something that would go on a BleachLaw vision board, but here I am, having served on the ABA TECHSHOW Board, sharing the tips and tricks that allow me to have a robust practice, provide excellent client service, and bake cookies. And while I'm not trying to impose my definition of bliss on you, how could one not find bliss in cookies?

Barbara Leach is the managing attorney at Barbara Leach Law where she works with her longtime paralegal and associate attorney. Originally an overworked, dispassionate complex commercial litigator at an 1,100-attorney national firm, she is now passionate about resolving conflict with minimum impact on her family law, bankruptcy, and business clients. She is a past president of the Central Florida Association for Women Lawyers, an inaugural fellow of the Florida Bar Leadership Academy, and has been recognized in both the *Legal Elite* and *Super Lawyers* publications. Her claim to fame (other than being a dog mom to the ChiLAWhua and baking kick-ass cookies) is helping lawyers to embrace technology in ways that improve their efficiency and bottom line. To that end, she is chair of the Orange County Bar Association's Technology Committee, chair of the Florida Bar Solo/Small Firm Section's Practice Management Conference, and has served on the 2017 ABA TECHSHOW Planning Committee, one of 10 people responsible for planning the largest legal technology conference in the world. Learn more about Barbara at www.bleachlaw.com.

Lesson 31

● ● ● ●

HOW TO AVOID FRICTION IN THE FAMILY WHEN YOU WORK FROM HOME

SUSAN CARTIER LIEBEL

At the moment of commitment, the entire universe
conspires to assure your success.

— GOETHE

Working from home can be an amazing experience if it is planned correctly—and an unmitigated disaster if it's not. More importantly, if handled *incorrectly* there can be a lot of friction in your home. Why? Because, while your spouse and kids go off to work and school to then come home to their "sanctuary," you are carefully and thoughtfully converting your sanctuary into a work space for a finite number of hours each day. This is a major psychological challenge.

I have worked from home for more than a decade, so it's fair to say I have a pretty good idea of what works and what doesn't; what lines to draw and what lines not to draw to keep you sane and your work time and space respected by your family. I also know there is an unspoken assumption that never really goes away: If you are working from home, you are always available for something. Some even go so far as to think you're not really working simply because they can physically see you, or you take a break for lunch and watch the news, or you decide it is a sweats and T-shirt day. This unspoken assumption, and sometimes resentment, never really goes away. Never.

SO, HOW TO DO YOU PLAN FOR SUCCESS?

First, it is key to have a dedicated space that includes your computer, phone, and a door that can be both closed and locked. Psychologically, you need to know that once you enter your work domain you are working. And your family needs to know this, too. I always keep my door open, though, so when it is shut, *no one* even knocks, never mind enters, unless the house is on fire. This might be harder with kids under age 10 running around if they are not in school or day care, but we'll assume for this Lesson, they are out of the house Monday through Friday.

Second, keep a shared calendar (without divulging confidential information) so that your spouse and kids (if they are old enough to access) know your workday, which includes conference calls, court calendars, appointments, "power hours," and more. I can't tell you how nice it is to have your spouse ask at dinner how your meeting was or tell you they waited to call you because they saw you had a conference call at a certain hour.

Third, let your immediate and extended family know your "power hours"—those hours of the week when you are drilling down to work, write briefs, research and do not want to be disturbed. Mine is every morning, especially Mondays. I've trained my family to never call or text unless it is an emergency. It takes time for your family to learn this because of the assumption mentioned above – "If you're home you aren't really working."

Fourth, set up definitive work hours. This can be very hard when you carpet commute because it is so easy to get up early and "go to work," so easy to finish dinner and run to your computer to work or just check that "one thing," especially if you need to connect with someone and they are in a different time zone. But this is where *you* need to be disciplined. Your home is *your* sanctuary, too. When your spouse is home and your kids are home, it needs to be family time, sanctuary time. This is probably the hardest part of working from home because it is incumbent on you, not your family, to be disciplined enough to turn it off. It is much easier to leave an outside work environment, unwind during your commute, walk into your home, kick off your shoes, and know the work day is over, than it is to get up from your desk, leave your office, shut the door, and not open it until the next morning. This is quite simply *the greatest challenge*. And to put things in perspective, when my son was five years old, he got very mad at me. All he ever saw was me working at the computer as I readied the launch of Solo Practice University. He was angry. Finally, I asked him why he wouldn't give me a hug. He said, "Because you love the computer more than you love me." Out of the mouths of babes.

The benefits of working from home are numerous. The possibility for familial friction is very, very real for the reasons stated above. But forewarned is forearmed. I've successfully navigated the landmines and reaped the rewards for more than a decade. You can, too.

Susan Cartier Liebel is a lawyer-turned-entrepreneur, founder and CEO of Solo Practice University®, the only online educational and professional networking community for lawyers and law students who want to create and grow their solo/small firm practices. She was an entrepreneur mentor for LawWithoutWalls.org for many years; and a member of the Advisory Board for the innovative Suffolk School of Law – Institute on Law Practice Technology and Innovation; an attorney who started her own successful practice right out of law school; an adjunct professor at Quinnipiac University School of Law for eight years teaching law students how to open their own practices; a sought-after speaker and columnist; and a contributor to numerous legal publications and books offering both practical knowledge and inspiration. Follow Susan on Facebook, Twitter, LinkedIn, and Google+.

Lesson 32

● ● ● ●

TO ERR IS HUMAN, EVEN FOR LAWYERS.
IT'S WHAT YOU DO AFTER THAT COUNTS.
PAULA LITT

There's no crying in baseball.

— *Tom Hanks* as *Jimmy Dugan* in *A League of Their Own*

We all make mistakes in real life. And real life includes our law practice. Most mistakes will not be fatal to our current job, let alone our future career. They may, however, erode confidence—not just our confidence in ourselves, but also the confidence others place in us. This is not necessarily right or fair. But, particularly in law firms, it is inevitable. Law firms worry about malpractice, losing cases and, worse, losing clients. They also weed out lawyers. Partners reviewing young associates and non-equity partners are asked: Has she got what it takes? Can you rely on her? Mistakes figure prominently in the answer.

The truth is this: How we handle our mistakes counts as much, if not more, than the mistakes themselves. This is especially true for women lawyers in law firms. Women are still seen as interlopers in a man's world, and as lawyers who will inevitably leave for "work-life balance." Law firms remain challenged. The numbers of women compared to men remain skewed at the partner level despite years of parity in law school classes. We cannot allow our mistakes and how we handle them to feed the narrative. So, here are a few tips from one who has been there and survived to tell the story.

Don't Panic. With luck, you will discover your mistake before someone else does, ideally in the quiet of your own office while reviewing a document or preparing for a meeting or argument. Sometimes you discover your mistake when your adversary points it out. Sometimes they are kind, and sometimes not. However your mistake is revealed to you, your first reaction may be a sinking feeling in the pit of your stomach.

But hold on a minute. Are you sure you actually made a mistake? Review the facts with a cool head. If possible, get a second opinion. More than once in my career I have thought I screwed up, only to have a colleague (usually one of the male variety) look at the same facts and reach a different conclusion. The point here is not to rationalize away the mistake. Rather, it is to be certain that a mistake was made before you rush to confession.

Determining whether you actually messed up is particularly important for women attorneys. This is illustrated by a study in which researchers Karina Schumann and Michael Ross set out to test the widely held belief that women apologize more than men. Their results were published in an article for the journal *Psychological Science* entitled *Why Women Apologize More Than Men: Gender Differences in Thresholds for Perceiving Offensive Behavior*. In the study, participants were divided into two groups by gender. Participants were asked to complete a questionnaire each night for 12 consecutive nights. The questionnaire asked them to describe three instances each day in which "you apologized to someone or did something to someone else that might have deserved an apology (regardless of whether or not you apologized)."

The researchers found that while the women did apologize more than men, they were also more likely than men to perceive behavior as offensive and therefore requiring an apology. Once the researchers controlled for the number of instances perceived as warranting an apology, there was no significant difference in the frequency of apologies between men and women. Women just had a "lower threshold" than men for what constitutes offensive behavior. A second study by the same researchers found that women judged offenses more severely than men, and the severity of that judgment predicted the extent to which an apology was deserved.

Here's the point: While some mistakes are clear as day, a lot of what we lawyers do is not black and white. It entails arguments, judgments, and strategy. The study described above suggests that it is at least possible that women should exercise caution before concluding that they, indeed, made a mistake.

Calmly assessing the situation is thus the critical first step. Did you *really* make a mistake, and if so, how important was it in the grand scheme of the matter? Did you blow a deadline for producing documents or getting a draft brief to the partner you are working with? Did you cite a case that had been overruled, miss a case you should have found, or mischaracterize a case you cited?

Own it. Once you know it, own it. Whether you report to a senior associate, department head, partner, or client, you need to tell them. No one wants surprises, and there is nothing worse than having them find out from someone else. How you approach the situation influences how the mistake (and you) will be perceived. Part of being a great lawyer is the ability to remain calm under pressure—or at least look like you are, even if you are quaking inside. Fessing up is a good test of that skill. Report the mistake along with your proposal for how to fix it. For example, can you file a corrected or amended brief or ask (preferably with self-deprecating humor) for a pass from opposing counsel?

As the partner in charge, I may not agree with your suggested fix, but I will appreciate the fact that you have proposed one and are not simply making your mistake my problem (which, of course, it is). Whatever you do, do not blame someone else for it (including – indeed, especially – a staff person), or suggest that someone else shares the blame with you—even if it's true. Blaming others transforms what should be a transitory event into what might be viewed as a fundamental character flaw. If you develop a reputation for throwing your co-workers under the bus, you will find yourself with a dwindling pool of co-workers willing to work with you.

You can express that you are sorry the mistake occurred. Some people feel that apologizing diminishes them, and they never do it. And some people (mostly young women, in my experience) say "I'm sorry" so often and for such trivial matters that it reflects poorly on them. Save it for when an apology is warranted, say it once and move on. Over-apologizing may be motivated by the best impulses of politeness and deference. But in the hard-scrabble world of law firms, over-apologizing, particularly for women, may only diminish the apologizer in the eyes of others, signaling everything from insecurity and self-doubt to powerlessness.

Learn from it. While a mistake will be forgiven the first time it is made, it will leave an indelible impression (and not a good one) if repeated. Repetition suggests that you are not listening, you do not care, or you are not smart enough to recognize the mistake in the first place. Learning from it requires you to figure out how it happened so that it will not happen again. Did you have a system of checks and balances? Where did it break down? Were your instructions and expectations clear? If someone you were relying on dropped the ball, you need to address it with them in a constructive manner, together figuring out what to do so it does not happen again. This is tricky stuff. Those who report to you will fear that they are in trouble. In word and deed, you must communicate that is not the case. But ignoring the problem will only lead to repetition.

Mistakes happen, even to the best. Understand them, deal with them, learn from them. And move on.

Paula Litt has spent her career litigating complex business disputes in courts across the country. She is a frequent author on legal issues and has spoken on litigation topics to the American Bar Association, the American College of Business Court Judges and the Illinois Institute on Continuing Legal Education, among others. Paula has been recognized by *Super Lawyers* (on its lists of Top 10 Illinois lawyers, Top 50 Illinois Women Lawyers, Top 100 Illinois Lawyers) and as a Leading Lawyer. She has received the highest ranking in Chambers USA. In July 2018 she was honored as a Role Model by the Harvard Law Society of Illinois. As a young attorney she joined three other lawyers to found Schopf & Weiss, a Chicago-based litigation boutique which had a successful 28-year run. Paula is now a partner in the Chicago office of Honigman LLP. Paula is a graduate of Harvard Law School. She holds an MA from The University of Chicago and received her bachelor's degree, *summa cum laude*, from The Ohio State University. Learn more about Paula at www.honigman.com.

Lesson 33

● ● ● ●

STOP AND SMELL THE ROSES
DIANE R. McGINNESS

Mistakes are the usual bridge between inexperience and wisdom.

— PHYLLIS THEROUX

As far back as elementary school, I dreamed of going to law school and becoming a lawyer. As far as I knew, none of my school friends was even remotely interested in the law or becoming a lawyer. Years later, after graduating from law school and while working as a young lawyer at a firm on the East Coast of Florida, my best friend since high school called me and, quite unexpectedly, said, "I am thinking of going to law school!" Fast-forward three and half years and my best friend's law school graduation was scheduled for a Saturday afternoon on the West Coast of Florida. My husband (who is also a lawyer) and I were both working on the East Coast and had made plans, along with my mother, to attend graduation and the after-party at her home.

A few days before the graduation, the head of the firm at which I worked announced that he was planning a Saturday meeting that required the attendance of all attorneys. The meeting was to be much like others held in the past: an all-day marathon meeting held on the weekend on short notice, with no definite end time, spent discussing all of the firm's cases being handled by the various attorneys. Much of the meeting would revolve around pending cases on which I had never worked and which were not part of my caseload.

My heart fell into my feet. The meeting was scheduled on the day of my best friend's law school graduation and I did not want to miss it. Before leaving my office that evening, I went to the head of the firm and asked if I could please miss this one meeting as it was my best friend's law school graduation, and I desperately wanted to attend. He refused to allow me to miss the meeting. I asked if I could possibly leave early so that I could fly across the state in time for the graduation. He also refused this request. Ultimately, he told me that I could leave around 5:00 p.m. because the meeting would probably be ending at that time.

In short, I missed my best friend's law school graduation. At about 5:15 p.m. on that Saturday I was allowed to leave the meeting. One of the other attorneys in the firm sped me to the airport so that I could make a flight to the West Coast of Florida, where my husband and mother were waiting to pick me up. Although I was thankful that I could at least be present at the after-party to celebrate my best friend's accomplishment, I was close to tears and angry that I missed her special day. It makes my blood boil to this day. In retrospect, I was not only angry at the partner, but a part of me was also angry with myself for not standing my ground and saying that I would not attend the meeting. Of course, my fear was that I would lose my position at the firm. I am sure many lawyers have found themselves in similar situations, especially as young lawyers.

Ultimately, I learned from this experience that the practice of law, or for that matter any work, should not be allowed to wreak havoc with your most important personal relationships. There are some moments in life that you simply can't get back. Your working life has to be reasonably balanced with your personal life.

In my life, I am blessed to have the most wonderful husband who has always role modeled the importance of working hard and playing hard, has always encouraged me to "stop and smell the roses" along life's journey, and who has been my strongest supporter in spurring me on to enjoy life to its fullest. Because of his constant support, I was able to stay home full-time when our daughter was born and to return to the practice of law more than a decade later, working part-time until our daughter left home for college. This decision was one that I have never regretted. I realized that the law would always be there, but our daughter would not, as she grew and went on to pursue her own goals. This realization applies equally to other loved ones and friends.

Although I was asked to return to work at the firm after our daughter was born, I did not take that offer. I realized then that the philosophy of and atmosphere in that firm did not fit me at all. I figured out that for me to thrive, I need to be part of a law firm with lawyers who acknowledge the priorities of family and the importance of having a well-rounded life, including one outside of the office. I also came to the realization that I had the choice to work in an environment that supports a balanced life and allows me to keep in focus what is most important in my life. On a daily basis, I remind myself that I have been given one life to live, that life is short, and that it is important for me to stop and smell the roses.

Diane R. McGinness is an attorney practicing with Price, Hamilton & Price in Bradenton, Florida. Her practice focuses on civil litigation and appeals, primarily in state court, in the areas of insurance defense, personal injury, motor vehicle negligence, premises liability and construction law. Born in Connecticut, she moved with her family to the East Coast of Florida when she was a teenager. She earned her B.A. degree in English, *with honors*, in three years at Florida Atlantic University as part of the Faculty Scholars Program. She earned her J.D. degree from the University of Florida. During summer breaks from law school she clerked at an insurance defense firm in Fort Lauderdale. After graduation, she began practicing law on the East Coast of Florida. After practicing law there for five years, she and her husband, who is a tax and estate planning attorney, moved to Sarasota, Florida, where they currently reside. They have one beloved daughter who is pursuing a doctoral degree in psychology. Diane is involved in the University of Florida Law Alumni Mentor program. When she is not practicing law and tending to her family, she is involved in the resurrection of her rose garden. Learn more about Diane at www.phpchtd.com.

Lesson 34

● ● ● ●

LET BOTH "MUSTS" AND "NEVERS" BE "MAYBES"

JULEE L. MILHAM

*If I were to wish for anything, I should not wish for wealth and power, but for
the passionate sense of the potential, for the eye which, ever young and ardent,
sees the possible. Pleasure disappoints, possibility never. And what wine is so
sparkling, what so fragrant, what so intoxicating, as possibility!*

— SØREN KIERKEGAARD

My journey to law school was peculiar. I was three months away from graduating college with a bachelor's degree in sociology and religion and had no
post-graduation plan. My heart was in the music industry, and one night a
musician friend's comment gave me this notion: I should go to law school so I
can protect all the cute band boys from the mean industry people who would
take advantage of them.

Sure, what else would a teenager think? The friend's comment came on a
Wednesday. I conferred with my parents when I saw them that Saturday, and
the LSAT was the next week. I knew no lawyers, and I didn't know what the
LSAT was or what law school was. I thought it was a trade school of sorts.
Although he denied it later, on first pronouncement, my father was under-
standably less than happy with this whimsical, expensive idea. He quickly
came around, but I realized I didn't really know what I was getting myself
into. When I pondered to my father, "What if it's not right for me?" he said,
"Go. If you don't like it, leave."

Go. If you don't like it, leave.

I know life decisions are rarely so cut and dried, and great authors have
written substantial libraries on the importance of planning, dedication, and
similar practices and qualities. Family obligations, financial constraints, and
numerous other life circumstances could make that statement sound flippant

and naive. But it's also profound. Not all efforts have to end in results. Not all endeavors are worthy of fruition.

I took my dad at his word. For me, it worked out. I wasn't trapped in or by my own mind; therefore, I wasn't stuck in what could have been (and for some are) miserable years. We all live with expectations of others. Some people have a natural influence on us, and some work at trying to influence us. Balancing and integrating those elements with our own autonomy and independent thinking is a perpetual dance, and at times a grueling one. What we don't need is our own expectations bearing down on us like a third person thwarting what may truly serve us in the end. We all need to get out of our own way.

That's not an indictment on the value of commitment or an exaltation of feelings. Commitment gives us context. It gives us stability when hard times batter us like a raft on a tumultuous sea. Commitment helps provide clarity. Despite what may sound capricious (and contrary) above, I do believe feelings should usually give way to commitments that otherwise continue to make sense. Feelings are sneakily unreliable. But they are also crucial. They make us human and empathetic, and they are irreplaceable as their own experience. But as a life gauge, they sometimes mislead us and sometimes leave us in ignorance. By "feelings," I'm not speaking of instinct or gut or passion. I'm speaking of that fluid sense of how something seems, whether in initial or unexplored perceptions or as a result of a change in circumstance.

When our impressions tell us we don't like something or someone, we tend to simply opt out. This makes sense. Why subject yourself to something you don't like or in which you see no value? But tantalizingly, behavior can change feelings. Actions allow us to explore those things we "feel" strongly about or that we are apathetic toward. And amazing things can happen when you let your experiences inform your feelings rather than insist your feelings determine your experience.

The band that first exposed me to the subculture that led me to law school included a member I simply could not abide. I thought he was full of himself, shallow, and purposely dumb. Over a few years, though, my paradigm became challenged. As I became close to his fellow band members, and he to my parents, I became bothered by my own prejudices. I got this gnawing sense that something had to give. I started wondering, if everyone I love loves him, maybe I'm not the know-it-all, but rather I'm the one missing the boat. So, although it made me *feel* unhappy, I decided to act completely out of sorts with how I felt. I invited him to dinner, and he accepted.

We ate. We talked. We laughed. We found things in common. I got insight into what made him who he was. And then I found that – along with his band members and my parents – I loved him, too.

Worlds away, eight years into my law practice, I saw an ad in the local bar newsletter that the circuit was holding a 40-hour training for people interested in becoming a traffic court hearing officer. It was free, and thus free continuing legal education. I had no ambitions of being on the bench, and I knew squat about traffic court other than my own tickets (or about anything quasi-criminal other than the questionable side of the entertainment industry). But that it was so foreign to me made it a bit of a kick. So, I went, although I had no particular interest in it. While it wasn't my intention, I was selected as an alternate hearing officer, and since it was an occasional gig that would not interfere with my practice, I accepted.

While my disinclination to being a judge never changed, that step out amplified my career in a way I never could have seen coming. Serving on the bench required me to develop life skills I never anticipated. It honed my ability to intently listen to what people say (and don't say). I learned how to cut straight to an issue and not be led astray from it. It taught me how to respond to hyper-emotion like Teflon rather than to naturally react and escalate conflict, which never works out well. That post led 18 months later to a second quasi-judicial position in small claims court that has been one of the greatest joys and grounding experiences of my life.

The tentacles of these positions expanded my view across all three branches of government. I've learned some of the inside worlds of law enforcement, government technology, court personnel, law-making, case management and statistics, budgets, dispute resolution, and other often-insular environments. More meaningfully, these assignments connect me to an incredible variety of people and their unique life challenges. Regularly touching on the worlds of others who do, contend with, and know things of which I am entirely clueless is both inimitably educational and consistently humbling. These roles have made me a better thinker and a better lawyer. Of most significance, they have bred gratitude in me.

Don't have an experience only because you think you must finish what you started. But supremely, don't forego an experience only because you don't see where it's going or how it will matter. Have as many experiences as you can. They surprise us and enrich our lives, and with each one, we become keener lawyers and more complete human beings.

Julee L. Milham is a sole practitioner who practices entertainment, intellectual property, and business law. She is AV-rated by Martindale-Hubbell and board certified by The Florida Bar in intellectual property law. She is one of nine committee members appointed to The Florida Bar's Intellectual Property Certification Committee. Julee is chair emeritus of the Florida Bar Entertainment, Arts, and Sports Law Section and authored *The Practice of Music Law in Florida* for The Florida Bar as well as *The Arts and the Law/ Florida* for Volunteer Lawyers for the Arts. She has taught entertainment law as an adjunct professor at Stetson University College of Law and often speaks regarding her areas of practice.

Since the 1990s, Julee has served on the Sixth Judicial Circuit of Florida as its small claims hearing officer and a civil traffic infraction hearing officer. She is an American Arbitration Association arbitrator and a certified mediator.

Julee studied comparative human rights and corporate governance at Oxford College of Law and is admitted to the Roll of Solicitors for England and Wales (non-practicing) as well as the Bars of Florida, New York, California, the District of Columbia, and several federal courts.

Out of a personal passion for poverty alleviation, Julee co-founded and co-chairs the New York State Bar Association's International Section Committee on Social Finance and Enterprise, formerly called Committee on Microfinance and Financial Inclusion. Its work has included consulting on international truth-in-lending legislation, transparency projects, and submissions to United Nations Commission on International Trade Law. Learn more about Julee at www.emusiclaw.com.

Lesson 35

● ● ● ●

LISTEN

KATE MITCHELL

Learn to be silent. Let your quiet mind listen and absorb.

— PYTHAGORAS

The practice of law is a skill, and like most skills, takes many years and experience to develop excellence. To develop competency in any field of law takes less time and less experience. There is a reason why we attorneys call what we do the "Practice." The Practice demands keeping at it, day-in and day-out; demands research, inquiry, and seeking answers and solutions from others; requires personal and professional examination; learning from one's mistakes; and pursuing excellence. We begin our career attending law school where we are taught the intellectual exercises of thinking logically, rationally, and reasonably; understanding legal constructs and concepts, and developing research skills. Law school gives one critical knowledge and exposure. It does not give you competency. For that, you must step out after your degree and begin somewhere to practice law, with the building blocks developed in law school.

I recommend that you not practice alone. If possible, begin with an apprenticeship. Find a mentor, preferably another woman attorney. If that is not possible, begin your practice surrounded by attorneys you respect, who you know are good at what they do, and can guide you when needed. Find a colleague with whom you can have lunch regularly. Practicing law is needlessly difficult without a guide to help you develop the competencies your clients require. You are seeking a combination of feeling competent and being centered in your own Practice. If you are reading this book, you are highly motivated, have developed or are developing competency in the areas in which you practice, and have been applying what you know to each client's issues from the initial consultation through successful resolution, growing professionally every day. Now, you seek a level beyond competency; you seek excellence.

On the road to excellence, I recommend you consider three things and then act upon each: (1) listen to yourself; (2) feel good about yourself in the profession; and (3) take time away from your practice.

Listen to yourself. The art of listening is also a practice. However well you listen today, learn to listen better every day. Listen to your clients, listen to your potential clients, listen to your colleagues, listen to whoever is across the table—and listen first and foremost to yourself. Scientists have hypothesized that the two sides of our brain, the right side and the left side, each performs different functions; yet each side communicates with the other. The left hemisphere of the brain is the side that we use developing our skills in logic, reasoning, linear thinking, thinking in words, and the like. The right hemisphere of the brain we use to develop artistic creations, think in sensitive terms, think conceptually, or "outside the box," engage our imagination, visualize skills, and the like. The right-brain/left-brain construct can be useful in discussing the Practice of Law. We use our left-brain skill set to look for and develop our logical, rational, and reasonable skills; to formulate and draw conclusions based on fact-finding and the written word with rational interpretation, precedents, traditional basis, and what is fair, just, and reasonable. This we learn in law school, and we put these skills to work in developing competencies in our legal practices.

Our right-brain skill set comes into play as we learn to listen, see, and sense the softest of whispers from within, and intuit what must be done to accompany the reasoned approach. It means taking time, whether that is a moment just before you decide on whether to represent a client or how best to proceed on behalf of a client. For example, a client calls with a legal problem within your practice area, outlines a fact pattern where you think you can be of use, is willing to sign an engagement letter, and agrees to a retainer. You schedule an initial consultation and meet with her. As you inquire as to the circumstances, there is a hint that the facts are not as clean or clear-cut as first indicated. Something isn't sitting right with you, but you can't quite pinpoint it. You just don't feel comfortable. Perhaps, there is more than one client and you don't like how they interact with each other. Or perhaps she writes a check and asks you to hold it for a week. If you take a moment and listen to yourself and what you are seeing, noticing, hearing, and sensing, you may decide that you should not take on that client.

Another example: You are meeting with a potential client for the first time—the legal issue will require considerable time in billable hours. She has the means to pay you and will give you a substantial retainer. You discover that she has been to another attorney, and that relationship didn't work out for her. You ask her to consider certain approaches on how best to proceed, and she rejects whatever you recommend. It is possible that this client and her legal issues would be financially lucrative to you. However, if you take a moment to listen to yourself, you know that it is not worth the financial gain, that this client likely will be dissatisfied with your work product, you will be frustrated with your interactions and her rejecting your advice and work. In each of these examples, there will be another attorney better suited than you to represent her. And by not taking on that client, you will be free to take on a client for whom you could truly be of use, who has a problem that you can solve and will happily pay you for your services. To listen as I recommend is another kind of Practice, but nevertheless so important.

Feel good about yourself in the profession. I want you to feel good about yourself in the profession. Feel good about where you are in your practice; feel good about how you have gone about getting to where you are today; and know that learning is good. Acknowledge what you have accomplished. Learn from your mistakes. Imperfection comes with the human condition. Learn from the past and look forward. Learning and feeling good about who you are professionally is essential to attaining excellence in the law.

Take time away from your practice. In order to attain feeling good about yourself, feeling centered and developing the ability to listen, you must take time away from your practice. Tap into that right-brain creative self you naturally have; give it a chance to develop. Do something every day that is for you. Sit and breathe; walk somewhere beautiful each day; play with your kids; paint; exercise; dance; do your sport—whatever is truly nurturing to you. Leonardo da Vinci believed that going away from where you are in your work was a good thing. To quote him: "Every now and then go away, have a little relaxation, for when you come back to your work your judgment will be surer; since to remain constantly at work will cause you to lose power of judgment. Go some distance away because the work appears smaller and more of it can be taken in at a glance, and a lack of harmony or proportion is more readily seen." Give your right-brain an opportunity to grow, develop, and communicate with and influence the left side of your brain. Foster your quiet mind and listen.

Kate Mitchell is a solo practitioner who established her law practice on Cape Cod and Nantucket in 1993, representing individuals, businesses, and families. Her practice focuses on construction law, real estate law, zoning and land use, business law, and estate planning.

After Boston College Law School and five years of practice in Vermont and the Boston area, Kate took time out to learn the construction business, working first in Boston's renovation market, learning – from the ground up – carpentry, the State Building Code, contracting, and business skills. Relocating to Nantucket, she combined her construction supervisor's license and her license to practice law, by founding Island Women Construction Company Inc., and with women as her crew, built 13 homes and completed hundreds of renovation projects. As a general contractor, Kate gained experience in administrative law, appearing before town officials and committees seeking permits for Island Women's construction projects. She also served on the Nantucket Finance Committee and the Zoning Board of Appeals, broadening her knowledge of town government, zoning, and land use laws.

Today, with hands-on experience, Kate brings practical business knowledge and construction experience to her law practice, providing her clients excellent legal advice, counsel, and representation. Kate's law office is located in a house built circa. 1770 on Cape Cod's historic Old Kings Highway in West Barnstable, Massachusetts, where she can be a weekend carpenter and where she is reminded daily that in providing her clients with excellent legal advice, counsel, and representation, in the pursuit of excellence, the practice of law requires "listening." Learn more about Kate at www.katemitchellattorney.com.

Lesson 36

● ● ● ●

FORGET THE MAP
KATHARINE H. PARKER

As you start traveling down that road of life, remember this: There are never enough comfort stops. The places you're going to are never on the map. And once you get that map out, you won't be able to re-fold it no matter how smart you are. So forget the map, roll down the windows, and whenever you can, pull over and have a picnic with a pig. And if you can help it, never fly as cargo.

– JIM HENSON

Why did you become a lawyer? I became a lawyer because I wanted a career, not a job. I wanted the fellowship provided by a profession. I wanted the opportunity to grow throughout my working life and to be intellectually challenged throughout. I wanted flexibility to remake myself, if I wanted, by pursuing new areas of interest. I wanted the security of knowing that I could always earn enough to support myself and my family. I wanted the power of knowledge and the skills to effect positive change for people and our community. After 25 years, I am grateful that I picked the right path for me.

It was not always easy. As the saying goes, "The law is a jealous spouse." The demands of a legal career require a delicate balancing act that can tip in dangerous directions. If one is not careful and constantly recalibrating, personal health and relationships can suffer. Reflecting back, there are a few words of advice I can offer based on personal experiences.

Play the long game. A legal career is life-long. There is time over the course of your career to work intensely and to step back and shift focus and reinvent yourself.

When I left my law firm partnership to become a U.S. magistrate judge, I was asked many questions. Why was I leaving a prestigious law firm and the perks that come with partnership for civil service at a salary of less than what associates make? Why would I accept a position that was not life tenure? The answer is that I have always envisioned my career in phases. First, I would learn, then I would earn, then I would give back. Because I like to solve problems and resolve disputes, being a magistrate judge was well-suited to my strengths. As a magistrate judge, I spend at least 50 percent of my time facilitating settlements in civil cases. Think about where you want your career to go. What roles do you envision for yourself? When in your career can you fill those roles? Give yourself time to enjoy each role and transition to the next one.

Focus on your life's priorities. Being a lawyer is part of your identity, but it is just one aspect of you as a person. Take time to be a parent, a child, a spouse, a friend. You will never regret time spent on important relationships— you will regret not spending time on them. You will never regret spending a half-hour per day exercising.

When I was a fifth-year associate, my husband and I decided it was time to start a family. I took five months off work after giving birth and then returned. About a month after returning, I felt overwhelmed with the responsibilities of motherhood and the amount of work needed on a new litigation. I went to the partner on the case to see whether I could get help on the case. She said that there was no budget to add another lawyer. I burst out crying because I did not know how I would manage. She handed me a tissue and said this was just a difficult transition time, and if I gave it another few months I would see that I could manage everything. She shared that she had experienced the same feelings returning to work after her first child. I went back to my office with some dread but feeling good that the partner had confidence that I could handle everything on my plate. I plotted out my schedule, made a task list, and tackled home and work tasks one day at a time. After a few months I learned how to balance. I became more organized at home and at work and stopped activities that were not my highest priorities.

Think of ways to streamline your life and of tasks that can be shifted to others, done less frequently, or not done at all. I learned that balance meant balancing over time, not balancing everything concurrently. There were times over the years when my balance tipped in favor of work or in favor of family or friends. There were times when I realized that I was not prioritizing properly and had to recalibrate. But I always remembered the advice of that partner, "Just give it time and you will figure it out." She was right!

What are your priorities? Are you saying "No" or, "Thanks for thinking of me, but now is not a good time. Please think of me later," to the things you don't want to do or don't have to do? Are you saying "Yes" to the wrong things?

Ask for opportunities. You are in charge of your career. If you want to take a deposition, first chair a trial, lead a negotiation, or run for a leadership position, you need to ask. The worst thing that can happen is that you don't get what you ask for.

As a second-year associate, I was assigned to work on a case that was headed to trial. I had never taken a deposition. I had not yet spoken in court. But I knew trials did not come around that often. I asked if I could examine some of the witnesses at trial. The partner and senior associate chuckled and said probably not. Undeterred, I worked hard to learn all the facts and relevant law. I made myself invaluable and then asked again, identifying specific witnesses who I thought I could handle. Grateful for my help and seeing that I was not only determined but also prepared, the partner granted my request. By not taking no for an answer and demonstrating my value, I got the experience I wanted.

What opportunities can you identify? Who do you ask? How do you demonstrate your readiness?

Reach. You didn't become a lawyer because you wanted everything to be easy. Ask to do things you haven't done before, so you learn and grow. This requires courage and a recognition that the first time you do something, you won't do it perfectly. You made it through law school and the bar exam—you can learn other skills by reaching past your comfort zone.

I reached when I asked to examine the witnesses. I had not been to a trial before, but I needed to learn, and I did.

How do you find courage to reach? What experiences in your life can you draw on? The first time you dove off the high diving board? The first time you rode a bike? The first time you drove a car? The first time you took a college exam? All of these experiences are times in your life when you reached and achieved.

Give back. All of us received help from others to reach our goals. Mentor younger lawyers. Take on a pro bono project. Join a bar association and contribute to the betterment of the profession. You will get back far more than you give.

One of the best experiences I had at my law firm combined pro bono and mentoring. I took on the defense of an individual who had been mistreated by the police. I asked a new associate to work on the case and told her I would "reverse shadow" her on depositions and at court conferences. We strategized together, learned together, knocked out the defendants' expert report, defeated summary judgment, and ultimately obtained over $100,000 as a non-confidential settlement for our client. The associate was more confident in her skills and well-positioned to take on harder assignments in the firm. I was the happiest of all, feeling like I was truly able to put my experience to use to help others.

How can you give back?

United States Magistrate Judge Katharine H. Parker was sworn into office for the Southern District of New York on Nov. 4, 2016. Prior to taking the bench, she was a partner at Proskauer Rose LLP where she practiced labor and employment law and chaired several practice groups. Before becoming a partner, she worked as an associate with the firm from 1993 through 2000. While at Proskauer, she had an active litigation career in cases involving the full gamut of federal, state, and local employment laws. She also litigated cases involving fair housing, civil rights, non-compete matters, contracts, and employee benefits disputes. While at Proskauer, Judge Parker was elected to be a fellow of The College of Labor and Employment Lawyers. She has been consistently honored in various listings such as *Best Lawyers* in America and New York *Super Lawyers*.

During her career, she has been actively involved with the New York City Bar Association and has chaired both the Disability Law and Employment Committees. Judge Parker is also involved in pro bono and charitable causes, including the Michael J. Fox Foundation and Girl Be Heard. She was a recipient of the Fairy Godmother Award from Girl Be Heard and the Jeremy Epstein Award for Pro Bono Service from the New York City Bar Association.

Judge Parker received a B.A. degree, *cum laude*, from Duke University in 1989. In 1992, she received her J.D., *cum laude*, from Fordham University School of Law, where she was elected to the Order of the Coif. She was a Notes & Articles editor for the *Fordham Law Review*.

Lesson 37

● ● ● ●

PUSHING PAST FEAR AND FAILURE
ARTIE RENEE POBJECKY

*If you want to conquer fear, don't sit home and think about it.
Go out and get busy.*

— DALE CARNEGIE

Life is hard, yet success is harder. To succeed risks must be taken. Even when things go right and everything seems easy, those triumphs are often built on a foundation of failures, gambles, and numerous headaches. Part of taking risks is to accept and embrace failure. Fear did not stop Neil Armstrong from walking on the moon, nor did 1,000 failures prevent Thomas Edison from creating the light bulb. I admit I am always looking for the secret formula to triple my revenue and client base; ultimately, I am reminded, by those who have paved the way ahead of me, that I already possess the "secret."

The secret to my solo practice and business success is working on my business versus in my business. The key component of working on my business is developing meaningful contacts with business executives. As an introvert, this is not fun, yet I push through it and I have enjoyed the rewards. However, in doing so, I must attend events without knowing anyone, run for an election and lose, and even hire the wrong people at work. Despite the initial heartaches and rejections from each of these examples, in the end, my perseverance and determination reaped tremendous rewards.

As a new attorney, I quickly became dismayed with the practice of law and was on a mission to exit. Fortunately, an opportunity presented itself to help two young girls leave Cuba for a future in the U.S. I knew nothing about immigration law and had to admit my ignorance on an American Bar

143

Association group email list. Then a kind soul pointed me in the direction of the American Immigration Lawyers Association. Again, I had to seek help from strangers. I remember leaving my first immigration conference with a migraine headache. This new practice area was hard, both from an educational and mental standpoint. There were times I made mistakes, and I had to overcome my fear of failure by reaching out to my colleagues or taking a case despite the obstacles. At times, I was ready to give up and admit defeat. Now, over a decade later, I am grateful that I pushed forward despite these fears and failures. I am eager to learn and take on new practice areas within the immigration field.

Now, after switching to immigration law, I am enjoying business success. Yet, I felt something was still missing, and I wanted to become more involved in my community. Working in a rural area, I felt isolated from my immigration colleagues, and I wanted more. I remember sitting in my car, making countless excuses as to why I should not attend a local event of female business leaders. I was alone and knew no one. It was awkward and hard. As soon as I entered the building, I felt immediately intimidated by the success. I wanted to run, but my feet were planted to the ground. Instead, I made my way to a small group and mainly listened to them. I began to listen to their successes and felt overwhelmed. To this day, I remember leaving the event with a headache from the stress and fear. The following month, I returned and continued the charade until it became fun. I made meaningful and lasting relationships with the "successful" female leaders. Looking back, I realized that I stayed true to myself and did not bloviate my accomplishments. Instead, I asked a lot of questions and stayed engaged in the conversations. My cell phone was turned off and I sent "thank you" notes to the hostesses. Eventually, the hard work paid off and my connections turned into genuine friendships. I consider many of these women mentors and kindred spirits because they are a part of the secret to my business and personal success. Today, I enjoy walking through an event and recognizing colleagues, and I proudly sit on several community boards. If I stayed in my car because of my fears, I would have missed out on some wonderful friendships and opportunities.

Despite my "successes," I keep pushing myself. I cannot afford to become complacent. When I walk into a room of strangers, I continuously remind myself to smile, hold my head up high and exude confidence on the outside. My secret is that I am a ball of nerves, but with my smile and poise, no one else has to know. Yes, I have been snubbed on many occasions, and that is OK. When I enter a room full of strangers, I look for smaller groups or find someone else who is standing alone—often there is another introvert in the room. Another secret: If you appear to be enjoying yourself by smiling, then others will usually gravitate toward you. I also believe it is essential to pay it forward. I force myself to leave the comfort of my colleagues and search for newbies so that I can help them feel more comfortable. I am always impressed when someone reaches out to me. If you are attending a new event, feel free to contact the coordinator and introduce yourself ahead of time. Ask to volunteer before the event—it might create opportunities to meet others in a smaller setting, and the hostess will not forget your generosity.

I learned that courage was not the absence of fear, but the triumph over it. The brave man is not he who does not feel afraid, but he who conquers that fear.

— Nelson Mandela

I do not like failure or rejection. This is a possibility with each email I send, each task I attempt, and each proposal I mail. It is only later in life that I have embraced these rejections and accepted that the rejections are not of me personally. Instead, the timing may not be right, or the email may have gotten lost in the junk box. Despite being an introvert, I have pushed myself to speak at national conferences and it is heartbreaking when the feedback is not positive. Yet, constructive criticism is critical to my success. Rejection is valuable. It forces me to re-examine my approach. It prevents complacency, and it pushes my boundaries. I am always trying to learn and better myself, both personally and professionally. Keep an eye out for opportunities and JUST DO IT. Remember, the only thing holding you back is yourself.

I've been absolutely terrified every moment of my life and I've never let it keep me from doing a single thing that I wanted to do.

— Georgia O'Keeffe

So what fears are holding you back? I encourage you to write them down and set goals to tackle. Create a checklist with timelines. Is there an event you want to attend, a mentor you want to meet, or a conference at which you'd like to speak? Then do it—we will keep your fears and nerves a secret between us. While the journey may be bumpy, it will open new windows of opportunities that you may never have realized exist or believed could be attained. I wish you many blessings as you embrace your fears and push through them. Onward and upward!

Artie Renee Pobjecky is the senior partner at Pobjecky & Pobjecky, LLP, a global immigration and consulting firm. She is the immediate past-chair of the American Immigration Lawyers Association (AILA), Central Florida Chapter. Artie is a nationally recognized speaker and published author on immigration issues. She is a frequent lecturer at state and national immigration conferences and has appeared on local news and cable programs. She enjoys speaking at local events and educating the community about the nuances of immigration law. Her speaking engagements include the 2013-2016 and 2018 AILA National Conferences and the 2012-2017 Central Florida AILA Conferences.

Artie was recognized by *Best Lawyers* for 2016-2018 and as a Rising Star in the practice of Immigration Law by *Super Lawyers* in 2014. In 2017, she received an award from the American Immigration Lawyers Association, Central Florida Chapter for Outstanding Contributions to the Chapter.

Artie is active in her community. She is a board member and vice president of the Winter Haven Chamber of Commerce. Additionally, she is a council member and board member for GiveWell Community Foundation.

Artie received her Bachelor of Arts degree in political science from the University of Central Florida with minors in English and business. In 2001, she graduated from Baylor University School of Law with her Juris Doctorate. When not practicing law, Artie enjoys traveling with her husband, charity runs, and reading biographies of those persevering from their obstacles. Learn more about Artie at www.pobjeckylaw.com.

Lesson 38

● ● ● ●

THE POWER OF PUTTING YOURSELF FIRST
KRISTINE REED

*Life becomes beautiful when you learn to be as good to yourself
as you are to others.*

— AUTHOR UNKNOWN

A few years ago, and about 20 years into my career as a lawyer, I decided to start running. For years, I had been busy running my small firm practice, running my kids around, running errands, and running myself ragged—but I had never intentionally run anyplace! Yet, there's nothing like a bottle of wine, a best friend, and the promise of a race in an exciting destination to change all that. So, the next morning I laced up a dusty old pair of tennis shoes. About 10 minutes in, I vowed to never, ever do it again. The music blaring from my headphones was not loud enough to drown out all the questions my brain was hurling at me: Who do you think you are? Do you even know how far 10 kilometers is? Do you know the last time you ran was probably on elementary school field day circa 1980, and you were also terrible then? Don't you have a brief to write?

I spent the next few weeks nursing sore quads, shin splints, self-doubt, and exhaustion. But it turns out that as with most things, running does get easier if you keep practicing, and so I did. And then a strange thing happened that I hadn't planned on. And no, it wasn't that I became an outstanding athlete! Rather, I started to notice that I actually felt better on the days that I ran. I had more energy. I had a sense of accomplishment even when other things in the day were messy and hectic or just didn't go well. And as my physical stamina increased, so it seemed did my mental stamina. And I don't know about you, but I really needed that.

I'm friends with a lot of wonderful women who are also professionals. They work hard in their careers and care about doing a great job for their clients and their companies. But they are not defined by their careers alone. They balance their professional lives every day with the multiple other hats they wear as women: mom, wife, friend, mentor, advisor, volunteer, coach, chauffer, homework helper, short order cook, maid, and so on. I know the type because I am the type. You probably are, too. To top it all off, I'm also a perfectionist and I like to do things myself! It's hard for me to ask other people for help. I feel like I'm supposed to be able to do it all with ease, so I keep trying to do just that.

I know this isn't a lifestyle that is at all unique to me. But what I have found more and more is that each time I have a chance to sit down and "get real" with another busy working woman, we confess that our efforts to do and be everything for everyone have left us tired, stressed out, feeling overwhelmed, and struggling to keep all the balls in the air. We run ourselves ragged for our clients, our bosses, our families. We don't say "no" when asked to do something for someone else, even if it means giving up rare moments for ourselves. We routinely prioritize ourselves dead last, and that needs to change. But even if you are lucky enough to recognize that behavior in yourself, sometimes you know where you should go before you know the way, right? Things need to change...but how? That was me, and then one day I saw something that seemed like a solution to the problem of how to add myself to my daily mix of priorities.

There's a meme that floats around the fitness world to the effect of, "A good workout takes one hour. That's 4% of your day. No excuses." When I first read that, my cynical self actually did the math. Was that even right? Turns out it is, and pretty obviously so, but I had never thought about it in that way. I decided I deserved 4% of my day! I was worth it! And 4% was small! It didn't sound selfish or luxurious or even hard to achieve! Let's do it! Here I go! I vowed to run for an hour or enjoy that time sitting on my deck with a great book when Ohio weather allows. I vowed to do it every day.

The more I tried, the more I realized it was not as easy as that meme suggested. And that made me realize the full extent of my self-neglect. Now don't get me wrong. In my family, we work hard and play harder. We love vacations and we do a great job of planning them and taking those breaks. But those weeks away happen a couple times per year. It was the space between that I had committed to change. So why was I having so much trouble adding in a 30-minute run or a 45-minute yoga class to my day on a regular basis?

Why in reality was it so challenging to carve out just 4% of my day to do something for myself? In the abstract, that seemed easy to accomplish, but I found that like running, it takes some practice. I'm still working on doing this every day, but I'm getting better.

Being a sucker for a challenge myself, I hereby challenge you to make yourself the priority in your life for one hour each day. I'm not saying you need to run. The only rules are that your hour must be for you, and it must be intentional. So, don't try to count that shower you took or the trip to the grocery store without the kids. Those are good things, but not really what I'm inviting you to do. Do something for you that nurtures you and restores you. Start by thinking about the things you really love to do. The things you "get to do" as opposed to the things that you "have to do." The things you look forward to indulging in when you get to take a vacation from time to time. Take a walk without your phone, read a few chapters of that book you've had on your bedside table for months, crank up the volume, listen to your favorite music and go for a drive with no destination, call an old friend just to catch up, meditate, sit in nature, get some exercise, sip coffee outside your favorite café. You know what you like. Allow yourself to enjoy it, not just once per year on vacation, but every single day.

I think what you'll find if you accept the challenge is that when you are intentional about carving out a bit of time for yourself, you'll not only benefit your own physical and mental health, but you'll be a better version of yourself for all the people and activities that you spend the rest of your time on. Take care of yourself first so you can take care of everything else you have to do. There's untapped power there, and I think you're going to love it.

Kristine Reed is a partner with Miltner Reed LLC, an Ohio firm serving businesses across the state with its principal office in the Cincinnati suburb of Mason. She enjoys practicing in a small firm setting and having the opportunity to build lasting relationships with clients. Priding herself on being down-to-earth and approachable, Kristine wants every client to have a great experience and to feel at ease in her office. The clock is not as important to her as really understanding the needs and goals of her clients, and that understanding keeps clients coming back and bringing friends and family with them.

When she's not wearing her lawyer hat, Kristine and her high-school-sweetheart husband, Mike, enjoy spending time with their teenage children, Andrew and Lauren. They enjoy family road trips, finding the best beaches, cheering on Ohio State football, and the occasional guilty pleasure of binge watching the latest Netflix original while eating too much pizza. You might also find Kristine at a local or not-so-local 5K, 10K, triathlon or half-marathon, either running by herself, with friends and family, or with her favorite volunteer program that focuses on the importance of health and fitness in addiction recovery.

Kristine received her undergraduate degree *cum laude* from Miami University in 1993 and earned her JD, *with high distinction,* at Ohio Northern University in 1996. She has enjoyed practicing law for more than 20 years, plans to stick around for a few more, and is licensed in Ohio, Indiana, and Georgia. Learn more about Kristine at www.miltner-reed.com.

Lesson 39

● ● ● ●

SLOW IT DOWN

STEPHANIE SCARBOROUGH

In the quiet hours when we are alone with ourselves and there's nobody to tell us what fine fellows we are, we come sometimes upon a moment in which we wonder...what good are we doing?

– A.A. MILNE

As women in the legal profession, we are everything to everyone. Counselors, managers, mothers, partners, lovers, and leaders. We work at full pace from the time we wake up in the morning until we close our eyes. Even our weekend mornings are ever-filled with duties and commitments as we head off to our tennis matches, take the kids to soccer, or volunteer at our church or temple. We are always organizing, moving, and producing. The same is true for me in my business and law practice. For the past 18 years I've been focused on grinding out more work and growing my business, and it's paid off in tangible successes. What I haven't done, however, is slow it down. I've never been well-suited to a slow pace. I'm a grinder. Nonetheless, I have found my insistence on pushing forward actually works against me. Sometimes one needs to simply slow down to allow our brain to make the necessary connections. It is in these slower periods of relaxation or meditation that the best ideas and connections often come.

As an avid but relatively new cyclist, I am always training to improve my speed and overall fitness level. My trainer tells me that at least one ride per week must be a recovery ride. A long, slow distance ride helps the body recover from rigorous maximum output training. Too much intensity on a recovery ride compromises recovery. I recently completed a 56-mile ride. I started the ride with the intention of riding at a long, slow distance pace. When I checked my stats post-ride, I realized I spent two hours and 30 minutes in the highest heart rate zone. Seventy percent of my ride was firmly at or near maximum heart rate which my fitness app tells me is "historic." That historic ride nearly did me in physically as I pushed myself to the limit. I wasn't racing anyone. In fact, I had no one to impress or beat as I was riding solo. I just couldn't bring myself to slow down the pace and listen to my trainer. My inability to slow down was hurting my overall improvement and, that day, almost had me calling for a ride at mile 40 when I was physically spent. In cycling, we call this "bonking" when we've depleted all our stored energy and nutrition. In business and in law, we can't allow ourselves to bonk. Following the right nutrition and riding strategies can prevent bonking in cycling. If you follow the right strategies, you can also prevent "the bonk" in your practice.

For many years I've kept the A.A. Milne quote at the top of this Lesson on my desk to remind me that every day I should be striving to make a difference in the lives of others. Recently though, the quote has taken on a new meaning. "In the quiet hours when we are alone with ourselves..." How often do we have quiet hours? We need to give ourselves the time to reflect and contemplate. Because in the quiet moments, ideas and innovation are born.

As lawyers, our lives are often filled with chaos. Taking time to reflect can marshal our thoughts and help us take transformative action. Reflection can also slow us down, give us time to recharge, and prevent our professional "bonking."

Reflection does not involve a formal planning session, so don't break out the spreadsheets. I'm referring to mindful and purposeful quiet time. This quiet time can simply be down time. Turn off and recharge and just be in the moment. But let's be honest, as women lawyers we are typically Type A. We may start off our recovery time nice and easy, but before we know it, we're hammering it out and pushing ourselves once again. Slowing down is hard, but it is essential to optimize your mind.

How does one slow down? Time blocking! Block off some time for yourself this week to simply be alone in the quiet hours. Be prepared because for those not accustomed to quiet time, the reflection that comes during this period can make you feel uncomfortable and even vulnerable. Still, your time of reflection can be some of the most valuable time you build into your week. At first, just allow the thoughts and ideas to come. Eureka moments often happen when we are not directing our minds to search for them. Don't force your thoughts. If something brilliant comes, take the time to write the thought down. If no thoughts come, that's OK, too. With time, your mind will become accustomed to the quiet times. Just as your muscles must be conditioned to meet cycling or fitness milestones, the mind must be trained and conditioned to expect these quiet times.

When you're ready, you can begin to use this time to reflect on specific issues or goals.

Here are some questions you can reflect on:

1. Where is my business or career today?
2. Where do I want my legal career to go?
3. Is my work still fulfilling to me?
4. If not, how can I make it more fulfilling?
5. What does success look like for me, for my colleagues, and my staff?
6. How can I better support my staff, colleagues, or partners?

As you enjoy the quiet moments, you are likely to have a eureka moment where a previously unsolvable issue suddenly becomes clear and obvious. Be sure to record your ideas and findings as these are the gifts that result from reflection.

Reflection has aided my practice during a recent transformation. My reflection was focused on the broader question of resource alignment. I worried about the issue for several weeks, but it wasn't until I quietly reflected that my eureka moment came. I needed to re-evaluate and change my practice. What followed was a transformation that allowed me to spend more quality time with my family as I started to rebuild the practice I love.

Quiet, solo reflection is the candy bar that restores our blood sugar and heals the bonk. The long, slow distance days and those quiet moments exist to supercharge our minds and energize our spirits so that we can again take on the world. Give yourself time today for your own quiet hours.

Stephanie Scarborough is an attorney and business counselor to families, small businesses, and multinational corporations. After U.S. Armed Forces service, which included deploying for Operation Desert Storm, Stephanie gained exposure to the inner workings of a multinational corporation while working closely with senior executives. She transitioned into law and has been managing her own businesses for the last 18 years. She often relies on the knowledge she gained 'in the trenches' to counsel clients.

Stephanie's work with investors and small businesses allows her to provide in-depth counsel to new and emerging business owners. She enjoys working with business owners who face some of the same challenges she has faced in her business.

Whether working with multinational corporations, small businesses, or families, Stephanie cherishes her connection with clients and has been fortunate to build lasting professional friendships which now extend throughout the world.

Stephanie's career has been nontraditional starting with her military service, her status as a mature law school student with three toddler boys, and extending to the leadership of her successful law practice. Throughout her career she has relied on the tremendous support of her partner of 21 years and their three teen boys. Stephanie is also an avid cyclist and credits the sport with rejuvenating her practice, health, and personal life.

Stephanie is a graduate of the University at Buffalo Law School and is admitted to practice law in New York and Georgia. She manages Scarborough Law's offices in Jacksonville, Florida; Alpharetta, Georgia; and Thiruvananthapuram, India. Learn more about Stephanie at www.scarboroughlaw.com.

Lesson 40

● ● ● ●

DON'T RESIST...REINVENT
KAREN DUNN SKINNER

Just keep swimming.

— DORY IN *FINDING NEMO*

I was never supposed to be a lawyer. For as long as I can remember, I wanted to be a doctor. I went to university and studied life sciences: microbiology, chemistry, physiology, virology, pharmacology, and anatomy. In my third year, when my classmates were madly applying to medical schools, I had an epiphany. I loved the science (except organic chemistry), but I hated the competition and pressure. The thought of spending another few years competing against the same people to get into medical school, and then competing with them for another four years to get through medical school, was entirely unappealing. So, what should I do with my B.Sc.? Why not law school? No competition there, right?

At that point, I didn't know anyone in law school. I didn't even know any lawyers. It just sounded interesting (and there was no organic chemistry). I took the LSAT and discovered I apparently had some aptitude. *OK then*, I thought, *maybe it's not such a long shot*. I had no idea which law schools were good law schools. The internet hadn't been invented yet, so I couldn't do much research. Instead, I applied to schools in cities where I wanted to live. My main criteria were languages and skiing, and possibly an ocean. I picked McGill University because I liked Montreal, I would be close to ski hills, and I'd get to improve my French.

It turns out that first reinvention (i.e., from doctor to lawyer) was fantastic. I loved law school. I loved McGill. And I still love Montreal. After years of wandering, it is once again my home (selected, along with my lawyer husband, for the skiing and the French).

After graduation in 1993, I articled with Stikeman Elliott in Budapest. Articling is forced labor cleverly disguised as apprenticeship. It's a necessary evil for Canadian lawyers. I was extraordinarily lucky; I got to article in Europe and was called to the Bar in a private ceremony in a gorgeous room in the old Palais de Justice in Paris. I spent two years working for Stikeman in Budapest, learning Hungarian, speaking four languages every day, and skiing in the Alps and the High Tatras (seeing the theme?).

We represented the Hungarian government in the privatization of its electricity industry. My work revolved around the development of the regulations needed to support the new industry. It was fantastic work, but the hours were long. We regularly put in 36-hour stints at the office, ate all our meals there, and slept on cots in the basement. It was hardly a normal start to a legal career; I had far more exposure and responsibility than most junior lawyers ever get. I loved it, but it exhausted me. Time for another reinvention. I moved to London and started a Ph.D. in law at the London School of Economics.

Somewhere along the way, I reinvented myself again and became a mother. I'm not sure why I thought a baby and a Ph.D. would be compatible. It turns out, they weren't. My Ph.D. morphed into part-time, and then long-distance when we moved back to Canada.

The Ph.D. became harder and harder, and at the same time, my little side-hustle grew. I'd been helping out a friend, providing legal advice on his corporate finance deals across Eastern Europe. I realized how much I missed practicing law, so I set up a small private practice and worked from Montreal. I advised him on his multi-jurisdictional mergers and acquisitions, and drafted transaction documentation. When that work dried up, I applied my experience in regulatory and administrative law to education and developed a practice advising schools on corporate governance and risk management.

Eventually, I decided I wanted back into the world of BigLaw. BigLaw, however, didn't want me. Despite having a successful small practice, recruiters told me I was "too far removed from law." I'd been "out too long." So, what did I do? I reinvented myself yet again.

Together with my husband, I founded Gimbal, a Lean practice management consultancy. We trained in Lean and Six Sigma, change management, and design thinking. We adapted Lean business tools and strategies to the profession we know best, and now we work with law firms and in-house legal departments across North America. We teach LeanLegal® strategies to thousands of lawyers and the business and administrative folks who support their practice of law, and we conduct process improvement projects that make lawyers more efficient, productive, and happy. I'm back in BigLaw—but not the way I ever imagined.

The thing is, I could have looked at every one of my reinventions as a failure. Did I go to law school because I didn't think I could hack it in medical school? Did I start my Ph.D. because I didn't think I'd be happy practicing law forever? Did I quit it because it was too hard, or because, actually, I liked practicing law more than pursuing a doctorate? Maybe I set up my private practice because I didn't get a job in a BigLaw firm. Did I start my consulting business because (again) I didn't get a job in a BigLaw firm?

Perhaps that's what it looked like to someone on the outside, but not once did I see it that way. All of these "reinventions" were choices. They were experiments that took me in new directions. They were responses to challenges. And every one of them made me happy. I've built a life on reinventing myself. And I haven't even mentioned my eBay business or my silver jewelry sales or my stint as a professional editor.

Constant reinvention has proven to me that I'm resilient. I'm creative. I'm strong. In Lean thinking, every problem is an opportunity to improve. I think that's one reason why Lean appealed to me and seems to offer so much to our profession.

As lawyers, we are trained to look for solutions, to develop creative responses to new problems, to get results. We find opportunities and exploit them to the benefit of our clients. And yet, according to research, lawyers lack resilience. They avoid failure and change. We see this every day in our consulting practice. Even if the changes we develop with our clients improve their profitability or their performance, or their ability to compete, lawyers resist them.

My lesson to you is this: Stop resisting.

Embrace the hurdles thrown up in front of you. Accept every challenge and use your legal training to find your own creative solution. Roadblocks are not failures, they're opportunities to improve.

Karen Dunn Skinner is the co-founder of Gimbal Lean Practice Management Advisors. She's a Lean Six Sigma Black Belt and an attorney with over 20 years of experience practicing law in Canada and Europe. She combines her deep understanding of the legal industry with her training in Lean Six Sigma to provide practical solutions to the competitive and budgetary pressures on practitioners and clients alike.

Karen is an expert in Lean and process optimization. Her work adapting Lean's business improvement strategies to the legal industry has made her a recognized leader in legal practice innovation. She's taught Lean and process improvement to thousands of lawyers and legal professionals. And she's led process improvement projects in law firms and in the legal departments of government agencies and multinational companies across North America.

Karen was a member of the Quebec Bar for over 20 years. She has finally managed to meet all her criteria: She and her family live in Montreal, but spend winter weekends skiing at Tremblant and summer holidays learning to kite-surf in the Outer Banks of North Carolina. Learn more about Karen at www.gimbalcanada.com.

Lesson 41

● ● ● ●

FINISHING WELL

KIMBERLY STAMATELOS

There is a pervasive form of contemporary violence to which the idealist most easily succumbs: activism and overwork. The rush and pressure of modern life are a form, perhaps the most common form, of its innate violence. To allow oneself to be carried away by a multitude of conflicting concerns, to surrender to too many demands, to commit oneself to too many projects, to want to help everyone in everything, is to succumb to violence.

— *Thomas Merton*

In a few short months I'll be 62 years old. Actress Jane Fonda recently announced she is in her "last act" and although I hopefully have many more years of life, the finish line in my life as a lawyer is more clearly in view.

I want to chart an intentional path for my last act, living mindfully and finishing strong. As I begin the process, I'm struck with paralysis. Where do I want to go? A good starting point might be to reflect on where I've been.

I was the youngest in my law school class of 1981, graduating at age 23 and entering full-time law practice at age 24. I've had many legal jobs: in-house counsel, associate at firms of varying sizes, solo practitioner, and even senior partner at small law firms I've formed. I'd gone to law school to "help people." I was a kind and compassionate problem solver, a good listener and a lover of people from the time I was a little girl.

I launched from law school in one of the early waves of females deployed into the profession. Our role was clear—act like a man. After all, we'd been told that we were taking a spot rightfully belonging to a man with a family to support.

"Mr. Durant died right here at his desk," I was told by an associate at my first law firm job as he pointed to an office with an empty desk. It was as though Mr. Durant was a warrior who died in battle saving the world. I got the message.

I dove in as the only female in the firm's litigation section, charting my course as a workaholic, billing hours like a trooper. I silenced my inner voice and went full speed ahead, learning to be tough. Law school and the lawyers mentoring me convinced me that compassion was a weakness and aggression was a strength.

In my private life I paired with a man also constrained by his job, traveling for business five days a week. We married and had three children. What was wrong with me? I loved my babies, but I was obsessed with being a lawyer. I heard a new term called "work-life balance" so I joined the part-time work committee of the local bar association. The all-female committee soon disbanded with the summary finding that for women lawyers, "part-time" meant shoving all your full-time work into fewer hours and getting paid less.

I navigated as best I could with no women mentors to guide me. I'd race to Little League baseball games, editing documents in the stands while waiting for my son to bat so I could wave and give a thumb's up, and then race back to the office. I tried to be nurturing but I never took off my lawyer hat, often telling my children to "toughen up" instead of acquiescing to the sorrow of childhood bumps and bruises. Nannies were enlisted to help assuage working mother guilt. I'd try to mother my children when I came home exhausted from the office.

My marriage began to deteriorate so I stopped practicing law and tried staying home. I was an outcast among the other mothers. Their conversations were boring and their obsession with their children seemed unhealthy to me. I prepared spreadsheets for class cupcake volunteers and felt incompetent in my new role. I became depressed and like an addict who needed a fix, I yearned for the office.

At the same time, my lawyer father became ill at age 65 and came into my home for hospice care as he was dying. Toward the end he would hallucinate often saying he saw dead lawyer colleagues in the room. I wondered why the lawyers would show up to him instead of cosmic visits from loving relatives or his golfing buddies.

My father died, and I was divorced. Even though I wasn't working I was "imputed" with the income of a lawyer in the divorce. After all, wasn't that who I was? I had to recreate myself and start making money quickly and the most logical step was to reclaim my lawyer-self. When I went back to inhabit her skin, I noticed she was different. She was weary, having sustained a whirl-wind of life, tragedy, and brokenness.

I set up a law practice focusing on family law and mediation. I'd experienced devastation similar to what my clients were facing. I encouraged clients to find healing, forgiveness, and compassion and decided to claim those things for myself. I still fought for clients' rights and equity, but I did it with dignity, calmness, and compassion for all.

I felt more authentic as a person and a lawyer. I began to write. I transported my brother diagnosed at that time with cancer to his chemotherapy appointments. I watched the IV drip, drip, drip of the drug infusing him with life. The writing did the same for me. Each moment in the chair typing was life-giving, healing, rebuilding, and renewing myself.

I wrote and self-published *The Compassionate Lawyer* in 2014 and started speaking to lawyers about compassion in the practice. I mentored several lawyers and helped three women lawyers start their own firms. I encouraged lawyers to be compassionate problem solvers and for women lawyers to realize we should celebrate our unique gifts and skills as women.

I continue to practice, write, and teach about what I've discovered. Earlier this week I saw a woman lawyer in her first few months of practice aggressively tell off a male lawyer on the phone and then hang up only to burst into tears. "I'm such a wimp for crying!" she declared.

I told her that being tough and aggressive is uncomfortable for many women. We can do it, probably even more biting than men, but is it really who we are? The crying was undoubtedly from the adrenaline, but it was also a warning sign of living outside her authenticity. It hurt to watch her minimize her body's warning and I tried to tell her so, encouraging her to use compassion and dignity instead. I'm guessing it fell on deaf ears as it would have to me at her age when I'd set out to "make my mark" as a lawyer. But at least she is getting a message I was never told.

In my last act, I see a woman enjoying life, available to her three children for long talks instead of saying "I'll call you after this meeting." She is a compassionate, kind person to all she encounters. She practices law in an authentic way that is uniquely hers, until she decides it's time to stop. That woman will die as far away from her desk as she can get.

From the moment she walked into the doors of law school, her identity as "woman" and "lawyer" were permanently fused together. She's learned many lessons as a woman lawyer. She will claim her journey without regret but with gratitude for the wisdom she's gained. And most importantly, she'll live out her last act with compassion for herself.

Kimberly Stamatelos is in private practice in West Des Moines, Iowa. A graduate of Drake University Law School, Kim works primarily in family law, collaborative law, and mediation. She has been providing clients with compassionate problem solving for over 35 years. In addition to having had various positions in legal practice, Kim developed a mediation firm in five states in the Midwest and is a former vice president of training and development of Jams/Endispute.

Kim wrote and self-published *The Compassionate Lawyer* which set forth seven ways lawyers could bring more compassion to their law practices. She was named Drake University Law School's Alumna of the Year in 2015, in recognition of her work in the legal profession. Kim's second book is *The Spirit Filled Practice.* She has also published the Kindle book, *Shared Parenting With Your Former Spouse in Iowa.* All of Kim's books are available at Amazon.com.

Kim is the mother of Danielle, Courtney, and Clint and a Mini Goldendoodle Yogi, named for Kim's love of practicing yoga. Learn more about Kim at www.attorneymediate.com.

Lesson 42

● ● ● ●

WOMEN AND MENTORING: WHY PROFESSIONAL RELATIONSHIPS MATTER

MICHELLE R. SUSKAUER

As you grow older, you will discover that you have two hands,
one for helping yourself, the other for helping others.

— *AUDREY HEPBURN*

When I was a child, only three percent of lawyers in the United States were women. Now, in Florida, 38 percent of attorneys are women. And I write this shortly after having been installed as the 70th president of The Florida Bar, and only the sixth woman to serve in this role. Even so, we have a long way to go to achieve pay parity and increase the number of female equity and managing partners.

One of the most important ways that I have helped myself, both personally and professionally, is to seek the advice of mentors. I began my career as an assistant public defender in Palm Beach County where, on my first day of work, I met Scott Suskauer, who became an important mentor to me as I learned to manage complex criminal cases. Scott and I later married, opened our own practice and worked together for 18 years. He stresses the importance of being nice to everyone, from courtroom staff and clerks, to judicial assistants, attorneys, and clients.

My father, Alan Rosenkranz, and aunt, Sherry Hyman, have also been incredible mentors. They taught me the value of making meaningful connections, taking initiative, and being kind and compassionate. My father could talk to anyone, never came empty-handed and always followed up. My Aunt Sherry is an attorney in Jupiter, Florida. She urged me to join voluntary bar associations and get involved in the legal community. Early in my career, I joined the Florida Association for Women Lawyers (FAWL), where I found an incredible group of women who became a source of support and friendship.

Although technology has allowed us to be more productive, we are tethered to our phones, tablets, and computers around the clock, which has caused increased stress in the profession. My mentors have taught me to slow down and do things I enjoy—working out, baking, and spending time with family and friends. Women are so hard on ourselves, and I am no exception. As a working mother, I had to give up the idea of perfection. It is important to do the best that we can, but occasionally, just trying to do our best is enough. Throughout the years that my daughters were growing up, I had to rely on help from our family, friends, and community. Even now that they are in college, I feel that I have truly balanced home and work when I do not completely collapse at the end of the day!

Women are often underestimated, face negative stereotypes, and feel that we must work harder to prove ourselves in the profession. We are judged on our appearances as well as our work product; however, I do believe that women have an advantage in legal careers—we more naturally make connections with people.

Attorneys have the daunting task of helping those who are disadvantaged, and we are charged with leaving our communities and world in a better state than when we found it. We tend to have high cognitive reserves, are people-pleasers, competitive, critical thinkers, perfectionists, and we are fiercely independent. As mentally capable as we are of success, we should not isolate ourselves. In a modern profession plagued by mental health and substance abuse issues, one of the healthiest ways to combat stress and find fulfillment is by giving back to others.

Mentors act as role models, provide guidance, and listen, instilling a sense of competence and well-being. Mentoring comes in many forms. Virtual mentoring, for example, is a great option for lawyers with limited schedules or who work in remote areas or from home. Reverse mentoring pairs newer attorneys with more experienced ones, so that each person has something to teach and learn. Mentoring circles are also becoming more popular. This is a facilitated group put together around common goals or concerns, such as single parenting, and allows for a support system to develop in addition to professional guidance.

Sponsorship has become increasingly prevalent. In a 2016 *Business Insider* interview, Sylvia Ann Hewitt, CEO of the Center for Talent Innovation (CTI), relayed, "A mentor gives you friendly advice. A sponsor is senior in your organization or world and has the power to get you that next job." Sponsorship is a higher form of mentorship that requires timely investment in a protégé. A sponsor promotes visibility, makes introductions to leaders, gives critical feedback, encourages risk, and advocates for their protégé as they advance in the profession and, in exchange, is rewarded with excellent performance and loyalty.

Mentoring and sponsorship are particularly important for women. The 2017 Bentley University study, *Mentorship, Sponsorship, and Networks: The Power and Value of Professional Connections*, states that women with sponsors are more likely to be promoted, receive raises, and be assigned high-profile tasks. Further, CTI research shows that "85 percent of mothers (employed full-time) who have sponsors stay (in their profession), compared to only 58 percent of those going it alone." Mentees and protégés can be found within your firm, in law schools, or in voluntary bar organizations.

According to the publication *Women Want Five Things* from CTI, women typically want five things in their careers: they want to flourish, meaning they have a measure of control and the ability to self-actualize; they want to be intellectually challenged; they want their work to have meaning and purpose, including improving lives through social justice; they want to attain financial security; and women want to empower others and be empowered. The organization's executive summary of *Women Want Five Things* states, "Women seek sponsors: senior colleagues who are willing to take a bet on them and advocate for their next big opportunity. They also seek protégés: high-achieving junior colleagues who deepen their capabilities, extend their reach, and burnish their brand."

If women in the law are going to equalize the profession, both mentor and sponsor relationships are essential to this cause. That being said, these professional relationships must be organic and authentic. When this occurs, we can change the legal culture for the better. A February 2016 study funded by the Hazelden Betty Ford Foundation and published in the *Journal of Addiction Medicine* shows that attorneys have a high prevalence of substance abuse and mental health issues, and new attorneys are now being affected at higher rates than older ones. Mentors and sponsors must play a key role in recognizing warning signs early, asking the difficult questions to help these professionals find appropriate resources, and remain persistent in providing necessary ongoing support.

With one hand, I have helped myself by being a mentee and striving to live a balanced life; with the other, I encourage lawyers to become mentors and sponsors. There is a Jewish concept called *tikkun olam*, which means performing acts of kindness to improve the world. I learned from my mentors early in my career the importance of giving back to society through my involvement in my legal community and the community at large. Presently, I see an opportunity to advance the legal profession for everyone, especially for women. I will also promote a healthier, more balanced field, which seeks to close the justice gap and improve the criminal justice system. For this to happen, our profession must prioritize human development, and we must give back—not just to our clients, but also to ourselves and our peers. My mentors helped pave the way for me to lead the 106,000-member Florida Bar. I encourage you to build similar relationships and watch the powerful return.

Michelle R. Suskauer is a partner with Dimond Kaplan & Rothstein, P.A., in West Palm Beach, Florida where she heads the criminal defense practice group. Michelle is the 70th president of The Florida Bar and is the sixth woman to lead the Bar. She is the first former public defender to hold the office.

Michelle has been a member of The Florida Bar's Board of Governors since 2010 and has chaired the Board Disciplinary Review Committee, the Board Communications Committee, and the Annual Convention Committee. She has served as president of the Palm Beach County Bar Association and the Florida Association for Women Lawyers – Palm Beach County Chapter. She has also served as president of the board of directors of the Legal Aid Society of Palm Beach County.

Michelle earned a B.A. in communications from Boston University in 1988 and her J.D. from American University in 1991. She began her legal career at the Office of the 15th Circuit Public Defender in West Palm Beach, handling thousands of criminal cases. In 1997, she joined her husband, Scott Suskauer, at Suskauer Law Firm, P.A.

With more than 25 years of criminal defense experience, Michelle is also a nationally recognized and trusted legal analyst who frequently appears on television and radio shows. Learn more about Michelle at www.michellesuskauer.com.

Lesson 43

● ● ● ●

BUY A TICKET

LINDA S. THOMAS

You can't outwit fate by standing on the sidelines placing little side bets about the outcome of life. Either you wade in, risk everything you have to play the game, or you don't play at all. If you don't play you can't win.

— Judith McNaught

There's a wonderful joke that's been around for years about the poor man who goes to church every day and prays and prays, "Lord – please, please... let me win the lottery." His lament goes on for months and months, but to no avail. "Listen God," he says, "I know I haven't been perfect, but I really need to win the lottery." "I promise I will do better, if you just let me win." "I'll give some back to the church and to the poor. Just please let me win." "Help me out here. I have bills to pay." And on and on, week after week, but nothing. So, one day he shows up at the church, but instead of praying, he blurts out in anger, "God, you've disappointed me. I've prayed and prayed, and still nothing!" Completely exasperated, he storms out of the church vowing to never return. As he stomps out onto the sidewalk, the mighty clouds part, the rolling thunder booms, and a deep, loud voice resonates from the heavens and through the skies, "BUY! A! TICKET!"

I heard this joke for the first time several years ago from one of my dearest friends, Deb, who happens to be one of the best and most well-respected lawyers I know, when she was speaking to a conference of highly intelligent and motivated women lawyers about why we may find it difficult to advance in our careers to the places we want to be. Through her quick wit and mastery of the language, she reminded us it is no secret that the legal profession has historically been a man's world, and while it may be changing, it is still difficult for women lawyers to move up the ladder and achieve whatever 'success' is to us. In reality though, she went on to say, it may be at least partially our own fault. We all know that women must be assertive in our efforts to further our careers, make partner, or get appointed or elected to that office or position we want; but we also know that 'assertive' women may not be viewed in the best of light among our male peers. Deb's point, among other things, was that we cannot sit back, hoping that opportunity for advancement just falls in our lap; we must make it happen. More often than not, she suggests, opportunity presents itself in small, seemingly insignificant ways, and may be disguised as just more work for us to do. She encouraged us to look for opportunity or make that opportunity happen, then do what is necessary to achieve advancement toward success. In other words, she says, "Buy a ticket."

Back in 1997, I was a brand-new lawyer trying to start my legal career in a small city in Oklahoma—not a small town, but certainly not a large city, either. After 20 years of teaching public school (which becomes more relevant as this goes on), I decided to go to law school. Upon graduating from law school and passing the bar exam, I found it difficult to break into the legal world, especially in a place where I was literally the only woman lawyer in town (well, except for the few who were in-house counsel for an oil company headquartered there). I had zero luck with resumes and interviews in the all-male law firms, so I finally just hung out my shingle and hoped for the best. Then an opportunity (if you want to call it that) did actually fall into my lap. Fortunately, as it eventually turns out, the local county bar association customarily elected the newest attorney as its president—certainly not as any particular honor, but rather because no one else really wanted the position. That serendipitous event turned out to be the first step toward my success as a solo practitioner and how I became the president of the Oklahoma Bar Association. And here's how:

Remember my teaching background I mentioned? Well, teachers are great at projects, right? Men attorneys, not so much. So, during my year as president of the county bar association, we did several community projects – blood drives, toy drives, food drives, free legal answers on Law Day, Bowl for Kids' Sake with matching T-shirts – everything except a bake sale, I think. (I had more time than clients back then.) There was a bit of arm-twisting and maybe some shaming, but in the end, most of our members joined in.

Now here's the 'fortunate' part of that: Because of all the community service projects we did that year, our county bar association was recognized as the Outstanding County Bar Association of the Year by the Oklahoma

Bar Association. On behalf of our county bar association, I got to accept the award presented at the OBA Annual Meeting by the OBA president. The story gets better, I promise.

About that same time, Melissa, who turned out to be my first "woman lawyer" friend and mentor, was the president of the Oklahoma Bar Association (only the second women to serve in that position since the inception of the OBA). Guess what: She, too was a former school teacher. Recognizing talent (or maybe just tenacity) when she saw it, she encouraged me to run for the OBA Board of Governors position for my district when it came open that year. Without thinking much about it, I just did. And that started my years of service to our state bar association. And all the while, my private practice was steadily growing.

Fast forward, 15-plus years. Following in the footsteps of Melissa and Deb, now two of my dearest friends and mentors, I too served as the president of the Oklahoma Bar Association in 2017—the sixth woman to serve in that position. I also have been fortunate to have served in many other leadership roles in the OBA and was recently appointed as the out-of-state lawyer liaison on the State Bar of Texas Board of Directors. I have been the recipient of a variety of awards and recognitions and have served on various boards and committees in my community. And as new opportunities continue to present themselves, I "buy a ticket" whenever I can.

I say none of this to brag, but rather to emphasize that after almost 25 years of practicing law, I now have a huge network of the "best women lawyer friends" who have, from the very beginning of my career, encouraged me to "Buy a ticket." I give them the credit for my successes. I would not be where I am now without each of these wonderful women who lead by example, give really good advice, encourage others, and are simply there to share a glass of wine and say, "I hear you!" I suspect that behind every successful woman lawyer is a network of women lawyer friends who champion their success and the success of other women lawyers. To all of mine, I say "Thank You."

TAKEAWAYS:

- Surround yourself with those women who know you don't have to blow out someone else's candle for your own light to shine; but more importantly, be one of those women.
- When the opportunity presents itself, never miss a chance to "Buy a ticket!"

District Court Judge Linda S. Thomas was elected as district judge of the 11th Judicial District, State of Oklahoma in November 2018, after having been in private practice in Bartlesville, Oklahoma for almost 25 years. She served as president of the Oklahoma Bar Association in 2017 and as its vice president in 2009. She has also served on the OBA Board of Governors, the Professional Responsibility Commission, and has served as chair of the Leadership Taskforce since 2007. She's been a volunteer for Oklahoma Lawyers for American Heroes, Legal Aid of Northeastern Oklahoma, and Oklahoma's Free Legal Answers program. She's a benefactor fellow of the Oklahoma Bar Foundation, a Young Lawyer Division Fellow, and an Oklahoma Life Fellow of the American Bar Foundation.

Judge Thomas is the recipient of three OBA President's Awards for excellence in leadership and outstanding service. She is a recipient of the prestigious Mona Salyer Lambird Spotlight Award and the Oklahoma Bar Foundation's Gerald B. Kline – Jack L. Brown Distinguished Service Award.

After having taught public school for 20 years, Judge Thomas received her law degree from the University of Tulsa. She's a member of the American Bar Association and a life fellow of the American Bar Foundation. She is a member of the Washington County Bar Association, and is active in her community, having served on the boards of several local organizations. She is also a member of the Bartlesville First Church where she is on the board of trustees and serves as part of the children's ministry team.

Lesson 44

● ● ● ●

CONNECTION THROUGH VULNERABILITY
MICHELLE THOMPSON

Vulnerability is the birthplace of innovation, creativity, and change.

— BRENÉ BROWN

It is important to connect with people. Not only in our personal lives, but also professionally. Establishing connections with our clients, colleagues, and co-workers not only impacts our "bottom line," it is imperative for deriving joy in our professional lives. And often, the only way to truly connect with another is to open yourself up to them. We must reveal layers of ourselves to build connections. Often those layers are made up of our vulnerabilities. I think of it as "exposing our soft underbellies."

We are all aware of how to build connections in our personal lives: be present and truthful, sharing parts of ourselves that the rest of the world typically doesn't get to see. But in my legal practice, I found I was able to build trust, credibility, and lasting professional relationships by sharing my personal experiences with my clients. In particular, sharing with them the story of why I went into trust and estate law and my very painful personal story of what happened when my mom passed away. I was my mom's only child, raised in a blended family where my stepfather taught me everything from riding a bicycle to driving a car. He was, for all intents and purposes, my father. Except for when my mom died. At her death, after 44 years of marriage and "fatherhood," my stepfather told me he never did and never would consider me to be his daughter and that the family, as I knew it, was gone. Not only did I lose my mom – and my "father" – I also lost all the bequests and inheritances my mother had provided because my stepfather was my mom's trustee. He took everything that she'd provided for me. The debacle that ensued was and is still such a blur. It's hard to fathom that my mother's husband would have taken millions of dollars that were left for my benefit. But I've survived the quintessential blended family estate nightmare. Barely.

In my law practice, inevitably, I would receive clients who also had complex family dynamics. I guess it was the universe's way of using my awful personal story to me help protect others from having to endure the same pain and heartache. Because I had a compelling story, I would share it with my clients. They could sense my vulnerability. They could sense that I cared about ensuring their family would not have to endure the same fate. By sharing my story, I shared my palpable passion with them. My clients knew I cared!

Sadly, most people are afraid to share their vulnerability for fear of being perceived as weak or sappy. As a child, some of us received the message that sharing your inner fears and thoughts was not appropriate behavior. We were taught that stoicism and a stiff upper lip were the true signs of strength. Some us were told to always maintain your guard as people will take advantage of you; don't trust anyone; and keep your distance from people. Those destructive lessons build walls that make it hard for us to open up to others. However, the opposite is true. Revealing your deeper self to others is a sign of true strength and courage.

As lawyers, no matter your area of practice, we are in the "people business." It is imperative that we connect, show empathy and compassion, and show that we are people, too. Lawyers can be intimidating (as that's sometimes our job) and unapproachable. Lawyers want to be viewed as tough, unflinching perfectionists who have no "cracks in the façade." But as anyone with a Bar card knows, it's emotionally taxing to be a lawyer (to put it mildly). We must live up to such high standards and expectations—not to mention the stress of court and meeting hourly billing goals. All of which takes its toll over time.

We must keep in mind that often our clients are reaching out to us with some of their most troubling and embarrassing problems. It is an honor to have people come to us, trust us, and open up to us. This is what makes working with clients so rewarding. And the reciprocity of openness and vulnerability helps to disarm others through empathy and understanding.

I know it seems counterintuitive to share your "weaknesses" as a measure of your strength and as an opportunity to grow personally. And it may seem even more counterintuitive to see your "weaknesses" as a unique value proposition in your law practice. But try it and see if it doesn't make a positive impact. Revealing your vulnerability and connecting with clients on such a deeply personally level may be difficult, but it's worth it. We are hard-wired for connection. Only when we reveal exactly who we are, are we able to forge the bonds that make our professional and personal lives so rich!

Michelle Thompson works with individuals and families as an attorney and certified financial planner®. Her desire to work with people seeking financial guidance comes from a very personal place. In her last year of law school, her mom passed away unexpectedly. Michelle was faced with resolving her mom's complex estate while balancing the inherent difficulties of a blended family.

Born and raised in Atlanta, Michelle has always been an active member of her community. From 2004 to 2008, Michelle served as a firefighter and first responder with the East Point Fire Department. From 2009 to 2012, Michelle served as a city council-appointed member of the East Point Ethics Board. Additionally, Michelle has volunteered for both Hospice Atlanta and Project Open Hand.

Michelle received her finance degree from the University of North Carolina in Greensboro and her law degree from John Marshall Law School. Learn more about Michelle at www.atlantafinancial.com.

Lesson 45

● ● ● ●

THE GIFT THAT KEEPS ON GIVING
RENÉE E. THOMPSON

Fear can mean you are making progress.
Embrace it and use it to your advantage.

— *FRANK A. RODRIGUEZ*

My mother raised me to believe that I could do anything I wanted to do, and so I believed from a very young age that I was capable of accomplishing almost anything I put my mind to. Being raised with this positive outlook made it easier for me to see the silver lining during difficult times and to make the most out of the opportunities that presented themselves, because I was always taught to believe in myself and my abilities. I remember as a child she would read to me at night the story of *The Little Engine that Could*, filled with the power of positive thought and what you can do if you believe in yourself. In retrospect, that was quite an amazing gift that my mom gave me at a young age. After all, she taught me that if you believe it, you can see it, and if you can visualize it, then you can accomplish most anything. No matter whether it was schoolwork or one of many extracurricular activities, my mother always supported me and believed in me.

It was later in life, during my high school years, that I learned that my mother's encouragement of me as a child was because she was by her nature afraid to take risks while growing up, and she expressed to me her regret about not taking more risks during her lifetime. She once told me that fear of failure was paralyzing to her and prevented her from attempting things she really wanted to do. She explained how she promised herself as a young woman that if she ever had children of her own, she would raise them with the self-confidence and ability to take chances, and to believe in themselves and their potential. My mother wanted to ensure that if her child did fail at something, the failure would not be because they were afraid to try.

I am a grown woman now, and I work as an attorney and a mediator. In my legal career, I have encountered a great number of things that can create fear of failure: whether you've prepared a case well enough; how a jury or a judge will respond to an argument; whether your client will be happy with the outcome of a case (and whether you'll continue to have that client if they are not); and countless other fears that lawyers grapple with in the profession as a daily matter. And, as a female attorney, I have experienced many of the conflicts and expectations that go hand in hand with being a feminine professional in a historically masculine profession. The expectations of the profession, as well as those you sometimes place upon yourself, can be paralyzing if you let them be.

As I grew older, in more challenging times, I realized that believing in myself might not be enough. Even though I knew I was capable, I knew I could, but sometimes I didn't know how to do something I wanted to accomplish. After all, there are many skills we learn to master throughout our life, some of which seem beyond our reach at times.

I recall in my undergraduate studies I would see successful professional women and think, how will I ever become what they are with the level of proficiency they exude? And one day in college, my favorite college professor looked at me and said, if you don't have it in you now, then "fake it till you make it." I asked her what she meant. She explained that there are times in everyone's life when they do not believe they have it in them to do something, but that modeling how someone else might do it can give you a boost when you can't find it in yourself. She was right. Sometimes pushing forward until your skills and your confidence catch up with you keeps you from inaction and ultimately from fear of failure.

My mother passed last year, and even though she is no longer here to advise me or to lift me up when I'm down, I still hear her voice pushing me on, telling me I am capable of doing whatever I set my mind to. That was one of her greatest gifts to me, and it truly is a gift that keeps on giving. So, when I am facing moments of self-doubt, or I'm afraid, or I'm unsure how to handle a task or proceed with some plan, I try to remember my mom and my mentor. I try to remember to be strong and brave, and if that doesn't work, I look for someone who is a model of what I am trying to do or become, and then incorporate what I believe makes them special into a new approach to the task at hand. These lessons have served me well in my life and in my profession, and I think they translate to anyone who is looking for the confidence to move forward even in times of self-doubt. I owe so much of my happiness and success as a professional and as a person to those two amazing women in my life. Thank you, Joyce, for teaching me in college so much that has helped me to understand so many things essential to leadership. And thank you, Mom, for your love and support, and for always believing in me and helping me to believe in myself. Because while I used to think I could, now I know I can.

Renée E. Thompson is an active leader in The Florida Bar, and has received The Florida Bar President's Award of Merit twice while serving on the Bar's Board of Governors. She is a former president of The Florida Bar Young Lawyers Division, the Marion County Bar Association, and currently serves on The Florida Bar's Executive Committee, as budget chair and in her capacity as the Fifth Circuit Representative for Florida. She was the inaugural chair of The Florida Bar's Leadership Academy and was involved in its formation and implementation.

Renée has long had an interest in alternative dispute resolution and mediates disputes in both state and federal court with the firm of Upchurch, Watson, White and Max Mediation Group. She is a professor at the University of Florida Levin College of Law in the areas of practice management and technology. She has received The Florida Bar's Walter Crumbly Award from the Solo and Small Firm Section for her contributions in these areas. Renée established a reputation at a young age as a high achiever and has been listed among *Super Lawyers* since 2015, after the organization named her a Rising Star for five consecutive years. Learn more about Renée at www.uww-adr.com.

Lesson 46

● ● ● ●

MAKE AN ABSOLUTE UNCOMPROMISING COMMITMENT TO TAKING CARE OF YOURSELF
MARY E. VANDENACK

You will never find time for anything. If you want time, you must make it.

— CHARLES BUXTON

As a young lawyer, I was fortunate to have a mentor who pointed out that the legal profession can be consuming. A lawyer can be consumed not only by time demands, but intellectual and emotional challenges related to what they do. Regardless of a lawyer's practice area, a lawyer spends every day dealing with problems presented by others and constant deadlines related to dealing with such problems. Lawyers are always using significant energy to help others, meet deadlines, and deal with multiple conflicting priorities. My mentor suggested that those of us who engage in professions requiring constant output of energy need to be committed to practices and making the time to restore our energy and keep ourselves well.

I had a friend early in my career who had achieved significant success and climbed to a high-ranking corporate position at a Fortune 500 company at an early age. I used to work out with this friend. We were both runners and we ran races together. My friend's favorite statement was, "Never compromise a workout for work." I watched my friend live that despite a very busy career path and a family life. I decided to follow that example and I have lived that, no matter how busy I have gotten at times.

FINDING TIME

We aren't going to "find" time. We absolutely must make time. On a regular basis, make time to re-evaluate your schedule. If you hear yourself saying, "I just need some time to figure out how to find time," then you urgently need to make an appointment with yourself to evaluate your time use.

At your appointment with yourself, list all the items that you are committed to doing to take care of yourself. Prioritize them. Fill the self-care items into your calendar before you fill in anything else. Block them out a year in advance and prepare a calendar entry three to six months before the last entry reminding yourself to update the calendar to extend those personal calendar items further into the future. If you don't want others to see a particular entry in your calendar, write in "carpe diem," the Latin phrase for "seize the moment."

After you fill in your calendar with time slots for taking care of yourself, then fill in slots for family and friend commitments. Fill in sufficient blocks that you will be able to nurture your relationships and take care of family responsibilities. Avoid getting carried away in a manner that your calendar will become overwhelming.

Finally, consider your job. Identify all the things you must do on a daily basis such as answering emails, verifying time entries, and returning phone calls. Fill those items in on your calendar. Then, identify all those things you must do on a weekly basis. Fill those items in on the calendar. Then, identify monthly, quarterly, and annual things that you must do and fill those in. First, you will likely be amazed at how little time you have for anything other than such requirements. When you go through this exercise, you will have a clear picture of how you use your time. You will be able to make good decisions about what you can take on in terms of projects and meetings. Most lawyers keep taking every project that comes in and attend every event they are invited to.

STEPS TO TAKE CARE OF YOURSELF

1. **Block out time in your calendar**. Put wellness activities in first.
2. **Know what nurtures you.** Each of us has different needs in terms of what nurtures and feeds us and keeps us whole. And, that can change over time. Develop an awareness of what feeds you and makes you feel whole. Consider physical, financial, emotional, social, and spiritual needs.
3. **Make physical movement a daily part of your life.** During my early legal career, I was a runner. I blocked out time in my calendar for my runs. I found others who loved to run and could run at similar times. By participating in running groups, I could take care of exercise and

social needs at the same time. Not everyone likes running or the gym, but I very much encourage any woman lawyer to make physical activity a part of daily life. If a traditional workout doesn't appeal to you, walk, take up ballroom dancing, Jazzercise®, or tai chi. You can kayak, sail, hike. Housework and yardwork are physical activity.

4. **Eat well.** Eating well should always be a priority. The legal profession is fast paced. It is easy to engage in stress-related eating or eat poorly at the many events and activities that you are expected to attend. Develop strategies to eat healthy no matter what is going on. Make a priority timeslot in your calendar for planning what and how you will eat.

5. **Maintain a social life.** Practicing law is consuming if you don't have a family. If you are practicing law and have a family, finding time for social connections can become nearly impossible. However, maintaining connections and having a supportive group of friends is a fundamental aspect of staying well. Often, you can combine social connection with other activities in which you are engaging for wellness.

6. **Get regular massages.** Massages are a great way to "put back in" some of the energy that you expend in taking care of others and dealing with challenges all day long. Early in my career, an occasional massage was a luxury, but I built it into my budget. Currently, I get a 90-minute massage once a week. I never miss. If I am traveling, I find a spa. Massages have positive physical and mental effects.

7. **Get a coach.** Consider hiring a life coach, a business coach, or a health coach. If you work for a large law firm with a wellness budget, inquire into whether you can get coaching services as a benefit. Different coaches have different skill sets, so establish specific objectives and seek a coach that will assist you in meeting them. If a personal coach is not currently an option, participate in an organization or group where you can receive support.

8. **Choose well when it comes to friends**. Seek out "soul group" friends. Soul group friends are the ones who are truly happy for your successes, accept you exactly as you are, know your dark side and love you anyway. Such friends are there for you in your darkest hours and care about you whether you are a successful partner or momentarily jobless. Find people who make you happy and who make you feel good about yourself. Spend time with them and avoid energy vampires.

9. **Create a lifestyle that is in sync with your values.** As an early adult, a wise person told me, "If your values and your lifestyle are out of sync, you will be miserable." When I was a partner at one particular law firm, as I turned onto the street that took me to my office, I would feel sick. That law firm's culture was not suitable to my value system. I left and started my own firm. I decided to work in practice areas where my values and my work were a match. To the extent I engage in community service, I pick causes about which I am passionate.

10. **Find balance.** I'm not fond of the phrase "work-life" balance. Using that phrase implies that work is not part of life but something other than life. Work is part of life—a significant part of life. If we love what we do, it's far less of an issue to "get out of work to get to my life." With that said, our work, our health, our family, and our friends all require attention and energy. The amount of energy that each aspect of our lives demands will vary at different times. When we are dealing with young children, health issues, or other significant life challenges, finding balance can be incredibly difficult. Sometimes it is nearly impossible for a period of time. In those moments, be aware of the energy that is being consumed, stay committed to self-care fundamentals, and continue to seek a path that allows you to feel balanced again.

You can have a great life as a woman lawyer that includes career success and personal happiness. It does take a commitment.

Mary E. Vandenack is founding and managing member of Vandenack Weaver LLC in Omaha, Nebraska. Mary is a highly regarded practitioner in the areas of tax, benefits, high-net-worth estate planning, asset protection planning, executive compensation, business succession planning, tax dispute resolution, state and local tax, and tax-exempt entities. Mary's practice serves businesses and business owners, executives, real estate developers and investors, health care providers, and tax-exempt organizations.

Mary speaks and writes extensively in her areas of practice as well as on law practice management and wellness. She is a commentator for *Leimberg Information Services* and frequently contributes articles for publication. Mary also writes a wellness column for the *Metro Monthly* in Omaha, Nebraska.

Mary serves as co-chair of the Futures Task Force for the American Bar Association Real Property Trusts and Estates Section. She serves on the American Bar Association TECHSHOW Board and is the incoming editor in chief of *Law Practice Management Magazine*. She has been named to *Fortune Magazine* Women Leaders in the Law, *Best Lawyers* in Omaha 2018, *Best Lawyers* in America 2019, and is AV-rated by Martindale-Hubbell.

An innovator in the integration of technology into the practice of law, Mary was named to the American Bar Association LTRC Distinguished Women of Legal Tech 2018. She won the American Bar Association James I. Keane Award and presented at TECHSHOW 2015 in recognition of her efforts in the area of e-lawyering. Learn more about Mary at www.vwattys.com.

Lesson 47

● ● ● ●

OVERCOMING THE OBSTACLE OF NAYSAYERS
WENDI WEINER

Look yourself in the mirror and ask yourself,
"What do I want to do every day for the rest of my life?" Do that.

— GARY VAYNERHCUK

One of the hardest obstacles I had to overcome when I decided to leave my decade-plus career in law was blocking out the negativity and negative thoughts that came from "naysayers." I define naysayers as the people who will watch what you do with intrigue and interest, wonder how you do (or did) it, but fail to offer a single encouraging word of praise. They will not support you, they will not congratulate you, and they will not approve of your career decisions.

Instead, naysayers will offer words of discouragement to derail you or make you believe that your decision to have your own law firm, leave the practice of law, or take your legal career in a different direction is not the "right choice"—or it is simply "foolish." Their negative statements will throw a wrench in your thought process and may even make you question your journey. Perhaps it is due to their own limitations in their lives or careers, but it is not for you to understand their "why."

Trust me when I implore you to just say "no" to the naysayers. They will not see the vision you see, and it isn't their responsibility to see it. It's your responsibility to live that vision and believe in it.

I want to share a story with you that happened to me—how I confronted one particular naysayer, what I learned from it, and how it changed my perception.

One of the first experiences I had with a naysayer in disguise took place at an entrepreneur event I attended on a Thursday after I had just made the bold decision four days prior to leave my 11-plus year career in law. I walked over to the coffee station at the event and was greeted by a guy in a dress shirt and navy pants.

"So, tell me about your business," he said. "What do you do?"

I chuckled. It had only been four days since I left law and plunged into full-time entrepreneurship.

Excitedly, I responded, "I'm a lawyer who actually left the practice of law on Monday after 10-plus years to follow my dreams of being a writer. I write resumes and LinkedIn profiles for lawyers and executives."

"Why would you stop being a lawyer to become a writer?" he asked. "That's just dumb! You will never make the type of money as a writer that you would make as a lawyer."

I was appalled, shocked, and humiliated. The only thing I could think of saying on the cusp in response was, "I gave myself six months to make this a reality, so we will see if it's possible."

I went home that day and for a good hour, I doubted myself and the plans I had for my entrepreneurial journey. I started to question what I was doing— was I making a huge mistake? Did this guy have a point? Would I ever be as successful as people thought I was as when I was a practicing lawyer?

Six months later, I re-introduced myself to that same guy, and he asked how I was doing. When I told him about being published in the *HuffPost*, *Forbes*, and multiple other publications, he inquired how I did it and if he could hire me to write his bio and website content.

The reality is that six months later, my confidence grew because I didn't give up or give in to the naysayer. I now look back at that day, that moment, that conversation, and I realize that you will always have naysayers, haters, and fewer people supporting you as you reach business success; but what matters most is how you see yourself. Being a lawyer does not automatically make us successful; but to the outside world it does. Laypersons perceive lawyers as successful, so when we tell them we have taken an alternative path in our profession, they automatically see that as questionable success. What I have learned over time is to use my situation and example of leaving the practice of law as a teachable moment for others to show them that yes, it can be done, and with great finesse, strategy, and incredible success.

More importantly, I stopped introducing myself to people as a resume writer and began to introduce myself as an attorney and personal branding expert. It's not that I wasn't proud of what I was doing; it's that I realized resume writing was only a small part of what I do as a professional writer.

When I began to really discover what my own brand was and how valuable it was, suddenly there was no longer the obstacle of naysayers in front of me.

I learned to take what was an obstacle and turned it around into both a lesson and my own teachable moment that I learned and grew from.

Wendi Weiner is an attorney, former college writing professor, and award-winning career and branding expert. Wendi has been featured and published in more than 50 major media outlets for her expertise in job search, personal branding, and resume writing strategies, including *CNN, HuffPost, Thrive Global, Forbes, Entrepreneur, Fortune, Business Insider,* and *Fast Company.* As the owner of The Writing Guru®, her trademarked namesake company, Wendi creates powerful career and personal brands for attorneys, top-tier executives, and business leaders. Wendi also serves as a contributing writer for *HuffPost* and *Thrive Global,* and as a content writer for *Inc. Magazine's* Content Strategies division.

A recipient of numerous honors and awards for her industry success, Wendi's leading recognitions include being named the #1 Resume Expert by Recruiter.com, Best Executive Resume Writer, Best Legal Resume Services, a Recommended Executive Resume Writer by Heller Search Firm, Top 25 Resume Site, and a Top 100 Career Blog.

Wendi's own career trajectory includes serving as a practicing member of The Florida Bar for over 11 years, working in BigLaw for a top national law firm and serving as a corporate trial attorney for a Fortune 200 company. Wendi entered the careers industry to follow her passion for writing and to help others achieve their own career dreams and success. For nearly three years, Wendi served on the board of directors for The National Resume Writers' Association. Her roles included serving as a director of industry to mentor new resume writers and as the president-elect and ethics chair of the organization to raise the public image of the organization and industry. Learn more about Wendi at www.writingguru.net.

Lesson 48

● ● ● ●

THE ART AND SCIENCE OF SAYING NO
JEANNINE WILLIAMS

*It's up to each of us to invent our own future with the choices we make
and the actions we take.*

– MICHELLE OBAMA

THE SCIENCE

Your brain is a fascinating organ. It only weighs three pounds and is uniquely divided into two hemispheres which process information in very distinct ways. My oldest daughter is a left-brained and right-brained person who can just as easily create beautiful sculptures as she can solve difficult calculus problems. Most of us are not wired this way. Many of us lawyers lean to the left. I lean to the left so dramatically, it's hard to stand up straight. I can barely draw stick figures and visualizing a highly decorated room gives me a headache.

As analytical as lawyers are, you would think the science of saying "no" would be easy. We are taught in law school to consider all sides of the argument and advocate for one or the other. We should easily weigh the pros and cons of "yes" versus "no." But often we find ourselves saying "yes" when we really want to, and should, say "no." Why is that?

YOUR BRAIN IS TRAINED.

Your brain is not automatically wired with a resistance to say "no." Women are taught from a very early age to be nice, quiet, and agreeable. We are taught to put others' feelings before our own. All of the external factors – our family, educators, friends, and the media – teach us that we should be selfless and supportive. If our spouses, our children, our colleagues, our friends are in need, we should do everything within our power to help.

Based on what I was taught, I rarely said "no" to anything for a very long time. If asked to help, I helped. If asked to fundraise, I gathered donations. If asked to lead, I led. At one point, I was actively engaged in the role of daughter, sister, wife, mother of two young daughters, friend, mentor, assistant city attorney, president of my local bar association, and board member of six organizations.

As much as I enjoyed helping, I did not want to be the award-winning volunteer at the expense of other very important roles in my life. Sound familiar? Feel free to insert mother, lawyer, wife, friend, daughter, sister, or any other role in place of "volunteer" in the preceding sentence to make it more familiar to you.

RETRAIN YOUR BRAIN.

The years of training can be unlearned. While there is nothing wrong with being helpful, the danger emerges when you continuously subject your own needs to the point that you frequently end up doing things that don't propel you toward your destiny. For most of you, if you are truly honest with yourself, you recognize that this is happening to you right now. I know this because dozens of my friends and colleagues have told me that they feel trapped into doing things they don't want to do because what they would like to do instead seems, dare I say the "S" word, selfish. Sometimes you want to relax instead of attending a client event (your boss gasps). Sometimes you want to take a theater class instead of joining the wonderful community board (society says, how could you?). Sometimes you want to further your career instead of starting a family (your mother says you're insane).

At this point we have to ask, do you want a future by default, or a future by design? I had to step back and look at my life to figure out what I wanted my life to look like. In that season, I decided to focus on family and work. I completed my terms on the boards and said "no" to another term. I said "no" to some very prestigious boards which did not have African-American members. Societal pressures told me to take the positions because they are not offered to everyone. My focus told me it wasn't the right time for me.

Once you decide what success looks like for you, it becomes easy to say "no" to things that interfere with what is important to you such as a meeting with a big client, your child's performance or game, dinner with your partner (personal or professional), or just a lazy weekend completing a puzzle (best weekend ever!). There is no right or wrong answer in what you choose as long as your answer moves you toward the future you design.

Once you have retrained your brain, it's time to work on your delivery.

THE ART.

Talk less, smile more. This is a line from my youngest daughter's favorite musical, *Hamilton*. It has become my internal mantra. I have given it a totally different context. Often, we talk ourselves into saying "yes" before our brain has a chance to tell our lips to move. As we are doing this, the other person is still talking, so we are missing what is being said. When this happens, you are not actively listening. (For more help with that, read "Lesson 35. How to Listen. Really Listen." in *50 Lessons for Lawyers: Earn more. Stress less. Be awesome.)*

You say "yes" before you know the extent of what yes means and what you have to sacrifice. Sometimes you say "yes" before the person has asked you to do anything. You have volunteered to do something you don't want to do before being asked. What sense does that make? Do not assume the ask is coming even if every time you see that person, they are asking you do to something. Sometimes you will get lucky and they won't ask. Then you smile.

SAY "NO." GIVE YOUR REASON. (SILENCE.)

You will not always get lucky. The ask will come. If what you are being asked doesn't fit into the future you have designed, say "no" and mean it. Don't apologize for it. Don't say you don't think you can. Don't say maybe later if you never want to do it. Say "no." Your reason may be that you are not interested, or you have another commitment, or the timing isn't right. Whatever the reason, state it once. Don't say anything else. If there is awkward silence, let it sit.

Many people underestimate the power of silence. There is a pull to fill the void. Don't give in. When I litigated, some of the best testimony in deposition came from sitting in silence. I asked a question. The witness answered. Silence. The witness added more—and then came the good stuff. The stuff that his lawyer told him not to volunteer. Silence is a powerful tool. Use it.

SAYING "NO" ISN'T EASY, SO PRACTICE.

I know you are thinking that's easier said than done. No one said it would be easy. It's hard to do, especially with people we care about or respect. Trust me, it takes a lot of practice. If you need to start small, do so. Say "no" when someone tries to sell something to you. Work your way up to saying "no" to small favors. Then, it's time to take on the big asks. You're not saying "no" to the person, you're saying "no" to the question. More importantly, you're saying "yes" to something you value more.

Practice even though you feel like a bad friend. Practice even though you think people will talk about you. Practice especially when someone is not taking no for the answer that it is. Think about it this way: Wouldn't you rather do something difficult for a few minutes than spend a week or a year honoring a commitment you never wanted to do in the first place? To this question, it's OK to answer "YES"!

Jeannine Williams is a government relations professional currently serving as St Petersburg, Florida's chief assistant city attorney. She is board certified by The Florida Bar in city, county, and local government law. She practices in the areas of ethics, public records, employment, disability, contracts, land use, litigation, emergency management, and elections law. She is also an adjunct professor at Stetson University College of Law.

Jeannine is the only African-American to have served as president of the St. Petersburg Bar Association, a voluntary bar with more than 1,200 members. She was also chair of The Florida Bar's City, County and Local Government Law Section. Jeannine was the recipient of the Florida Supreme Court Chief Justice's Leadership Award, Sixth Judicial Circuit's Pro Bono Service Award, and the William Reece Smith, Jr Public Service Award.

Jeannine received her undergraduate degree in business economics, *summa cum laude*, from Florida A&M University and her J.D from the University of Florida College of Law, where she was president of the UF Trial Team and a member of the UF Moot Court Team.

Jeannine is married to an extremely supportive husband, Alfred, and they have two amazing, confident teenage daughters, Jaylen and Alyssa. She is also a mentor, Sunday school teacher, and volunteer for several community service organizations. Learn more about Jeannine at www.stpete.org.

Lesson 49

● ● ● ●

THE FINE ART OF SURRENDER
J. KIM WRIGHT

*Surrender is a fine art that, like any art, requires practice and patience,
particularly given the power we've already surrendered to our personal will in
a vain attempt at flow control. The river has its own destination and will not
be dammed. We can choose to relax and float or struggle and sink. The only
difference is in how much suffering we will have to endure.*

— ROBERT RIVERSONG

Lawyers are known for their ability to get things done. We can be bulldozers, even when it stresses us out and takes a toll on those around us. We are strong-willed and proud of it. For most of us, "will" is an invisible, constant companion. If we want something done, we can MAKE it happen. We're the royal family of "Can-Do" and "No One Does Busy Better." We will work the long hours; we will do what it takes.

Even so, others sometimes do not respond as we would like for them to.

I have a lawyer friend who does amazing work. Having retired from her successful law practice, she designed a transformational program, hired marketing experts to provide the very best advice, and markets herself everywhere she goes. Yet, she doesn't have the level of business she wants.

Do you remember the insurance salesman, Ned Ryerson, in the movie "Groundhog Day"? Ned accosts people on the street and tries to sell them insurance. It is easy to imagine that even people who need insurance run the other way when they see Ned coming. Ned and my friend are trying to make something happen, using their will in a self-serving way that doesn't honor the flow of what seems inevitable.

A few years ago, I decided it was my year to *make* something happen. I reached out to some celebrities in other fields—authors, peacemakers, and healers who weren't lawyers, and who had international followings. We scheduled a series of joint events nearly every month throughout the year. They were excited to be better known by lawyers. I was going to reach the lawyers who were already in those more conscious communities.

I went to work. Other people went to work. We worked hard, putting in a lot of hours at our desks, creating websites, marketing campaigns, etc. I have taken all the internet marketing classes, know the tricks, know who to ask for help. We followed all the rules and – being the good lawyers that we are – pushed and pushed. We held conference calls at midnight and pitched everyone we knew. My will was in full force and it had the company of other lawyers to encourage its full expression.

One by one, the events fell apart or just didn't work out. My partner for the January event turned out to be someone who wasn't quite who I thought he was. I ended that association and our joint program did not happen. The co-leader of the February conference just up and cancelled, without discussion, a few weeks before the event. I spent the next year repairing relationships with the registrants who had made non-refundable airline reservations. I ended up with a big hole in a cross-country itinerary and had to spend money on hotel rooms no one would use.

Not listening to the flow of what was happening, we worked harder. We held the third event which was a financial disaster. Not only did we lose money, I paid more to be there than the participants paid for the workshop, while missing my nephew's wedding. The chaos of the event harmed a long-term friendship; years later, it is only beginning to recover. And, with the writing clearly on the wall, the next event was cancelled before it added to the mess.

All my will was wasted. I was exhausted. I was stressed. My resources were depleted. I wasn't having fun. I was working as hard as I ever had as a full-time lawyer and getting no positive results. Meanwhile, I'd gotten several spontaneous invitations to speak along the cross-country journey. I made a detour to Columbus, Ohio, which turned out to be one of my favorite places. Who'd have guessed? It was unplanned and evolved from a chance encounter. A visiting professor from Down Under invited me to speak to her classes in Ontario. In a synchronistic chain of events, I was interviewed for a podcast by the guy who had just been asked to find a speaker for a conference—they needed a holistic lawyer to give the keynote…in Australia! The dates exactly matched my open dates.

At the end of the year, I was reflecting on the fiasco of failed events. I noticed that those events I tried to will into existence were flops. Those events were focused on making something happen, including making me "famous" by association. The events which I allowed to unfold were much more fun, less work, and generally paid more.

I decided to embrace surrender. I can hear you thinking, "Surrender?!? Me?!? Never!!! This was not in the law school curriculum!" Take a deep breath. Maybe two deep breaths. Hear me out. Surrender is not a bad word. Surrender can be the same as "Go with the flow." Rather than fighting the current, I decided to embrace surrender as an experiment, to let my energy go where it wanted to go, and to ignore those demands of what I "should" do to "make" it happen.

Surrender became my practice. I stopped pushing and allowed things to unfold, and amazing things did start happening. Not only did I go to Australia that year, I was invited back, and I've been several times. (In 2018, more than a third of my income came from Australia.)

Soon, I was invited to South Africa for the first of many times. Europe was next. Eventually I added India to my itinerary. I've always dreamed of traveling abroad and I found myself circumnavigating the globe several times over the next several years. Amazing serendipitous meetings happened when I listened deeply and aligned with the pulse of life.

After spending three years focused on the pure practice of surrender, it seemed that I had learned enough to move to the next level. I was ready to experiment with my will again. I now see my will as the tool to help me on my path, a servant rather than a dominant force. When I am not clear about where to go, what to do next, I step back and contemplate. It may be that I take a walk or create space in my calendar to spend a few days in nature. I step out of the whirling tornado that is my life, and I find the place of calm where I can see how things are spinning. Then, I can work with the spin, not fight against it. (OK, I know I mix metaphors. Wind and water are part of nature and so is the flow that is my life. It helps me to think of that connection as I find my own flow.)

In my moments of deep silence and reflection, I can feel the flow. I can sense what is next and where I should be. When I discern a direction, I can ever so gently turn my will in that direction. Sometimes I might need to give it a push, but I'm pushing in the direction that life wants to go, working with rather than forcing.

I can tell when I am on track. My work is more efficient. It takes less effort for greater results. One well-placed phone call is worth a dozen random ones. Often, when I get clear about who I should talk to, the phone rings or an email pings and it is the exact right person. Knowing when to wait and when to push is valuable information.

Surrendering has taught me a lot about the rhythms of the universe and my place in it. My will is the tool to follow my path, a servant rather than a dominant force, in service of my bigger mission. I no longer struggle to make my dreams come true. I allow life to unfold in ways that are even better than I dreamed.

J. Kim Wright has been a pioneer in humanistic, relational approaches in law. Licensed in North Carolina in 1994, she has been on the cutting edge of most of the emerging models. From collaborative divorce practice to restorative justice to values-based contracts (and many others), she has practiced, pioneered, and promoted innovative models and ideas. These approaches have collectively come to be known as Integrative Law.

Kim is the author of two foundational books for the global Integrative Law movement, *Lawyers as Peacemakers* (ABA, 2010) and *Lawyers as Changemakers* (ABA, 2016) and is a contributor to *The Best Lawyer You Can Be* by Stewart Levine (ABA Law Practice Management, 2018). In 2009, the ABA named Kim as one of its first Legal Rebels, "finding new ways to practice law, represent their clients, adjudicate cases and train the next generation of lawyers." She also writes for periodicals at the intersection of conscious business and law.

Since 2008, Kim has been a nomad, traveling around the globe, building a network of integrative lawyers, coaching, consulting, and training hundreds of legal professionals. Kim is one of the founders and co-chair of the American Bar Association Dispute Resolution Section's Task Force on Relational Practice and was responsible for the conception and creation of the Task Force's Virtual Summit. She is a 1989 graduate of the University of Florida College of Law and has been a member of the North Carolina Bar since 1994. Learn more about Kim at www.jkimwright.com.

Lesson 50

● ● ● ●

KEEP THE DRAMA TO A MINIMUM
MICHELE ZAVOS

Don't waste time on what's not important.
Don't get sucked into the drama. Get on with it: don't dwell on the past.
Be a big person; be generous of spirit; be the person you'd admire.

– *ALLEGRA HUSTON*

The law is an adversarial system. There are winners and losers. Of course, that means that the legal process can be extremely competitive. It has been my experience that in general, men are more competitive in the legal arena than women. Being a woman almost automatically relegates you to secondary status in a law firm or in the courtroom. Subconsciously, male judges and male attorneys think women lawyers are not as good as male lawyers. Of course, this is not always the dynamic, but unfortunately, it often is. Men talk more, are given more attention, and are given more deference in almost all parts of society. Significant research in many areas of life confirms this to be true.

So, what does this mean for women attorneys? These issues are not limited to trial attorneys or those lawyers we traditionally think of as doing adversarial work. The entire legal system is adversarial. Accordingly, women attorneys often are put in the position of having to prove themselves equal to their male counterparts as part of their representation of their clients. So not only are women attorneys working for their clients, they are also going against the social assumptions that women are not as good as men in their field. Research confirms that women prize relationships and obtaining results, and work more collaboratively than men, whereas men generally prize winning and operating as individuals. This dynamic impacts women attorneys in the same way it affects women in all parts of society. A good example of this is collaborative law—in the geographic area of my family law practice, many more women are trained in and practice collaborative law than men.

Unfortunately, women often get sidetracked into proving points with male opposing counsels and get sucked into the competitive nature of trying to prove that as attorneys they are as good as the men they work against. Sometimes that competitiveness is necessary, but often it is not. When the competitiveness becomes paramount, the interests of the client may become secondary. When that occurs, attorneys' fees can skyrocket, and the case can become more about winning a point with opposing counsel than finding the best resolution for the client. Many attorneys focus on the minutia of the give and take inherent in a case rather than looking at the bigger picture of how to realistically resolve a case to their client's satisfaction. Sometimes it is far better to ignore a subtle "call to battle" or give in to opposing counsel's demands that have no substantive impact on your case.

In my almost 40-year legal career, I have seen attorneys argue over the most inane issues—like where a comma should be inserted that had nothing to do with the substantive outcome of a document, or exactly what word should be inserted in an order…again, where there is no relationship to the outcome of a case. These are distractions and are more about claiming a "win" than helping resolve a dispute. I have seen this far more between male and female attorneys than between female attorneys.

Don't be the kind of attorney who gets sucked into these types of battles. It is so easy to slip into, and so not worth it. Let the other side "win" for the purpose of keeping your clients' costs down, or moving the case along, as long as your client is not harmed by your "losing." Don't be the drama queen who needs to fight with opposing counsel over every issue. It is far better for your clients and for your reputation to be an attorney who gets things done.

Michele Zavos is a partner with Delaney McKinney in Chevy Chase, Maryland. She has been a pioneer for almost 40 years in creating legal protections for families headed by same-sex couples. Michele has given presentations on LGBT family issues to all kinds of audiences, both national and local, including other practitioners and judges. She has also written extensively on LGBT family law, sexual orientation and the law, and AIDS and the law. Her firm won the case of *Port v. Cowan*, which conclusively established that Maryland must recognize marriages between same-sex couples that are validly entered into in another jurisdiction.

Michele is a founder of the National LGBT Bar Association and a selected member of the National Family Law Advisory Council for the National Center for Lesbian Rights. She also served as an elected fellow of the American Academy of Adoption Attorneys and the American Academy of Assisted Reproductive Technology Attorneys from 2005 to 2015. She was named an "Angel in Adoption" in 2009 by Congresswoman Eleanor Holmes Norton, and has taught as an adjunct professor for the Women's Studies Program at the George Washington University and the Washington College of Law at American University. American University named her Outstanding Adjunct Professor in 1999. She and Eva Juncker, her former law partner, were named two of the best 25 divorce lawyers in Montgomery County, Maryland by *Bethesda Magazine* in 2013. She has won many awards for her work in the LGBT community, including being named by the *Washington Blade* as Best Lawyer in Gay D.C. in 2015 and 2018. Learn more about Michele at www.delaneymckinney.com.

ABOUT THE AUTHOR

A licensed attorney since 1992, Nora Riva Bergman is a law firm coach who understands the unique challenges lawyers face in the 21st century. She has practiced as an employment law attorney and certified mediator and has served as an adjunct professor at both Stetson University College of Law and the University of South Florida.

Nora has been a speaker at conferences for the American Bar Association, the Federal Bar Association, the American Academy of Adoption Attorneys, the National Association of Bar Executives, The Florida Bar, and other national and regional legal organizations. She also served for eight years as the executive director of a voluntary bar association with over 1,200 members.

She is certified in the Conflict Dynamics Profile developed by the Center for Conflict Dynamics at Eckerd College to help individuals and organizations learn to deal constructively with conflict. Nora is also a graduate of Villanova University's Lean Six Sigma Program and is certified in both DISC and EQ through Target Training International.

Nora received her undergraduate degree in journalism, *summa cum laude*, from the University of South Florida and her JD, *cum laude*, from Stetson University College of Law, where she was a member of the law review and served as a mentor for incoming students. She lives in Tarpon Springs, Florida, with her wife and their handsome son, a Samoyed named Cosmo.

CPSIA information can be obtained
at www.ICGtesting.com
Printed in the USA
BVHW030050080120
568855BV00001B/14/P